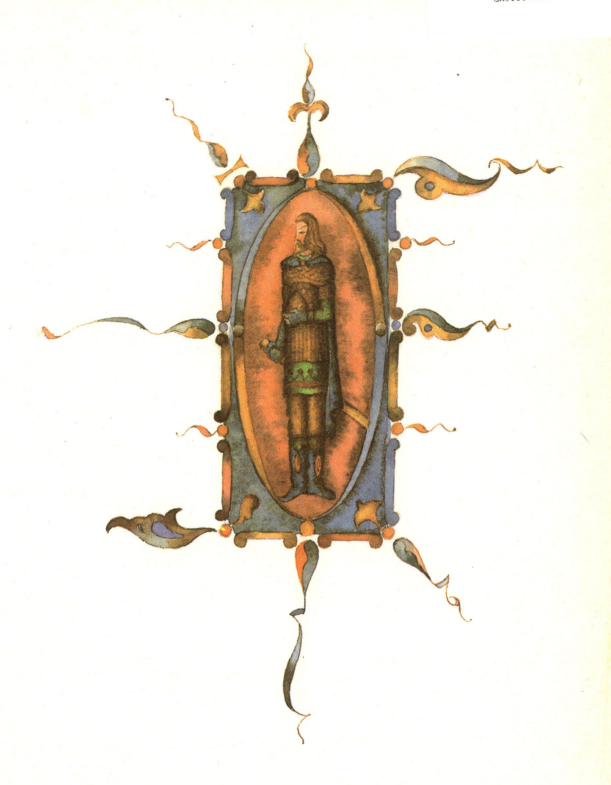

Raduga Publishers
Moscow

Alexander Pushkin
Ruslan and Ludmila

A Poem

Translated from the Russian by
Irina Zheleznova

Raduga Publishers
Moscow

Designed by *Mikhail Trubetskoi*

Illustrations by *Nikolai Dobritsyn*

А. ПУШКИН

Руслан и Людмила

На английском языке

English translation © Raduga Publishers 1986. Illustrated

Printed in the Union of Soviet Socialist Republics

ISBN 5-05-000674-0

RUSLAN AND LUDMILA

DEDICATION

For you, queens of my soul, my treasured
Young beauties, for your sake did I
Devote my golden hours of leisure
To writing down, I'll not deny,
With faithful hand of long past ages
The whispered fables.... Take them, pray,
Accept these playful lines, these pages
For which I ask no praise.... But stay!
For my reward – I need not seek it –
Is hope: Oh, that some girl should scan,
As only one who's lovesick can,
These naughty songs of mine in secret!

PROLOGUE

On seashore far a green oak towers,
And to it with a gold chain bound,
A learned cat whiles away the hours
By walking slowly round and round.
To right he walks, and sings a ditty;
To left he walks, and tells a tale....

What marvels there! A mermaid sitting
High in a tree, a sprite, a trail
Where unknown beasts move never seen by
Man's eyes, a hut on chicken feet,
Without a door, without a window,
An evil witch's lone retreat;
The woods and valleys there are teeming
With strange things.... Dawn brings waves
                           that, gleaming,

Over the sandy beaches creep,
And from the clear and shining water
Step thirty goodly knights escorted
By their Old Guardian, of the deep
An ancient dweller.... There a dreaded
And hated tsar is captive ta'en;
There, as all watch, for cloud banks headed,
Across the sea and o'er a plain,
A warlock bears a knight. There, weeping,
A princess sits locked in a cell,
And Grey Wolf serves her very well;
There, in a mortar, onward sweeping
All of itself, beneath the skies
The wicked Baba-Yaga flies;
There pines Koshchei and lusts for gold....

All breathes of Russ, the Russ of old!
There once was I, friends, and the cat,
As near him 'neath the oak I sat
And drank of sweet mead at my leisure,
Recounted tales to me.... With pleasure
One that I liked do I recall
And here and now will share with all....

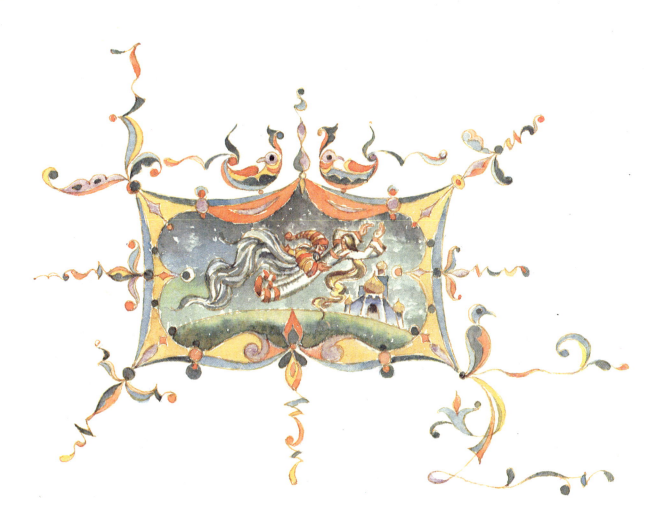

CANTO THE FIRST

The ways and deeds of days gone by,
A narrative on legend founded....

In princely banquet chamber high,
By doughty sons and guests surrounded,
Vladimir-Bright Sun holds a fête;
His daughter is the chosen mate
Of Prince Ruslan, and these two linking
In marriage, old Vladimir's drinking
Their health, a handsome cup and great
To his lips held and fond thoughts thinking.
Our fathers ate 'thout haste – indeed,
Passed slowly round the groaning tables
The silver beakers were and ladles
With frothing ale filled and with mead.

Into the heart cheer poured they, truly....
The bearers, bowing, solemn-faced,
Before the feasters tankards placed;
High rose the foam and hissed, unruly....

The hum of talk is loud, unceasing;
Abuzz the guests: a merry round.
Then through the hubbub, all ears pleasing,
There comes the gusli's rippling sound.
A hush. In dulcet song and ringing
Bayan, the bard — all hark him well —
Of bride and groom the praise is singing;
He lauds their union, gift of Lel.*

Ruslan, o'ercome by fiery feeling,
Of food partakes not; from Ludmila
He cannot tear away his eyes;
He flames with love, he frowns, he sighs,
At his moustache plucks, filled with torment,
And, all impatience, counts each moment.
Amid the noisy feasters brood
Three youthful knights. In doleful mood
They sit there, their great tankards empty,
With downcast eyes, the fare, though tempting,
Untouched; the goblets past them sail;
They do not seem to hear the tale
Of wisdom chanted by Bayan....
The luckless rivals of Ruslan,
Of love and hate a deadly brew
In their hearts hid, the three are too
O'erwrought for speech. The first of these
Is bold Rogdai of battle fame
('Twas he who Kiev's boundaries
Stretched with his blade); the next, the vain,
Loud-voiced Farlaf, by none defeated
At festal board, but tame, most tame
Mid flashing swords and tempers heated;
The last, the Khazar Khan Ratmir,
A reckless spirit, aye, and ardent.
All three are pale-browed, glum, despondent:
The feast's no feast, the cheer's no cheer.

---

* **Lel — the Slavic god of love.** — *Tr.*

It's over, and the feasters rise
And flock together. Noise. All eyes
Are smiling, all are on the two
Young newly-weds.... Ludmila, tearful,
Looks shyly down; her groom is cheerful,
He beams.... Now do the shades anew
Embrace the earth, e'er nearer creeping,
The murk of midnight veils the dome....
The boyars, by sweet mead made sleepy,
Bow to their hosts and make for home.
Ruslan's all rapture, all elation....
What bliss! In his imagination
His bride caresses he. But there
Is sadness in the warmth of feeling
With which, their happy union sealing,
The old prince blesses our young pair.

The bridal couch has long been ready;
The maid is led to it.... It's night.
The torches dim, but Lel already
His own bright lamp has set alight.
Love offers – see – its gifts most tender,
Its fondest wish at last comes true.
On carpets of Byzantine splendour
The jealous covers fall.... Do you
The sound of kisses, love's sweet token,
And its soft, whispered words not hear?
Does not – come, say – the murmur broken
Of shy reluctance reach your ear?
Anticipation fires the spirit,
O'erjoyed the groom.... But lo! – the air
Is rent by thunder, ever nearer
It comes. A flash! The lamp goes out,
The room sways, darkness all about,
Smoke pours.... Fear grips Ruslan, defeating
His native pluck: his heart stops beating....
All's silence, grim and threatening.
An eerie voice sounds twice. There rises
Up through the haze a menacing
Black figure.... Coiling smoke disguises
Its shape.... It vanishes.... Now our
Poor groom, on his brow drops of sweat,
Starts up, by sudden dread beset,

And for his bride – O fateful hour! –
With trembling hand gropes anxiously....
On emptiness he seizes, she
Has by some strange and evil power
Been borne away.... He's overcome....

Ah, if to be love's martyr some
Unfortunate young swain is fated,
His days may well be filled with gloom,
But life can still be tolerated.
But if in your arms, after years
Of longing, of desire, of tears,
Your bride of but one minute lies
And then becomes another's prize,
'Tis much too much... Quite frankly, I,
Were such my case, would choose to die!

But poor Ruslan's alive and tortured
In mind and heart.... O'erwhelmed by news,
Just then arrived, of the misfortune,
The Prince, enraged, turns on the youth.
The whole court summoning, "Ludmila....
Where is Ludmila?" thunders he.
Ruslan does not respond. "My children!
Your merits past high hold I.... Free,
I beg, my daughter from the clutches
Of evil. I am helpless; such is
Old age's piteous frailty.
But though I am too old to do it,
Not so are you. Go forth and save
My poor Ludmila, you'll not rue it:
He who succeeds, shall – writhe, you knave!
Why did you not, wretch, base tormentor,
Know how to guard your young wife better? –
Shall have Ludmila for a bride
And half my fathers' realm beside!...
Who'll heed my plea?" "I!" says the grieving,
Unhappy groom. "I!" shouts Rogdai,
And echoed by Farlaf his cry
And by Ratmir is. "We are leaving
Straightway, and pray believe us, sire,
We'll ride around the world entire
If need be. From your daughter parted
Not long will you be, never fear."

The old prince cannot speak for tears;
His gratitude is mute; sadhearted,
A broken man, at door he stands
And to them stretches out his hands.

All four the palace leave together;
Ruslan is ashen-faced, half-dead.
Thoughts of his kidnapped bride, of whether
He'll ever find the maid, with dread
And pain his heart fill. Now the foursome
Get on their restless, chafing horses,
And leaving dust clouds in their wake,
Away along the Dnieper make....
They're lost to sight, but Prince Vladimir
Stands gazing at the road and tries
To span the distance ever-dimming
As after them in thought he flies.

Ruslan, his mind and memory hazy,
Is mute, lost in a kind of trance;
Behind him, o'er his shoulder gazing,
The picture of young arrogance,
Farlaf rides, hand on hip, defiant.
Says he: "At last! The taste is sweet
Of freedom, friends.... When will we meet—
The prospect likes me well—a giant?
Then will blood pour as passions seethe
And victims offer to the sabre.
Rejoice, my blade! Rejoice, my steed,
And lightly, freely prance and caper!"

The Khazar Khan, his pulses racing,
In saddle dances, for in thought
He is the fair young maid embracing
Whose love he has for so long sought.
The light of hope is in his eye,
Now does he make his stallion fly,
Now forces him, the good steed teasing,
To rear, now gallops him uphill,
Now lets him prance about at will.

Rogdai is silent; with increasing
Unease his heart fills; dark thoughts chill
And burden him; he is tormented
By jealousy, and, all calm gone,
With hate-glazed eye, like one demented,
Stares sullenly at Prince Ruslan.

Along a single road the rivals
Rode on all through the day until
From east poured shades that night's arrival
Bespoke.... The Dnieper, cold and still,
Is wrapt in folds of mist.... The horses
Have need of rest.... Not far away
A track lies that another crosses.
"'Tis time to part," the riders say.
"Let us chance fate." So 'tis decided;
Each horse is given now its head,
And, by the touch of spur unguided,
Starts off and moves where 'twill ahead.

What do you in the hush of desert
Alone, Ruslan? Sad is your plight.

Was't all a dream—the bride you treasured,
The terrors of your wedding night?
Your helmet pushed down to your brows,
Your strong hands limp, the reins let loose,
O'er woods and fields astride your steed
You ride, while faith and hope recede
And leave you well-nigh dead of spirit....

A cave shows 'fore the knight; he nears it
And sees a light there. His feet lead
Him straight inside. The dark and brooding
Vaults seem as old as nature. Moody,
Distraught Ruslan is.... In the cave
A bearded ancient, his mien grave
And quiet, sits. A lamp is burning
Near him, a book lies on his knee;
Engrossed in it, its pages he
With careful hand is slowly turning.
"I bid you welcome, knight! At last!"
Says he in greeting, smiling warmly.
"Here have I twenty long years passed
Of my old age, and grim and lonely
They've been.... But now has come the day
For which, foreseeing it, I waited.
To meet, we two, my son, were fated,
Now sit and hear me out, I pray....
Ludmila from you has been taken;
You flag, you droop, by hope forsaken
And faith itself.... 'Tis wrong! For brief
With evil and its partner, grief,
Will be, I promise, your encounter.
Take heart; with strong, sound spirit counter
The blows of fortune, banish woe,
And, sword aloft held, northward go!

"He who has wronged you, O my daring
Young stalwart, is old Chernomor.
A wizard, he is known to carry
Young maids off to the hills. 'Tis for
Long years he's reigned there. None has ever
His castle seen, but through its door
You'll pass, I know, and end forever
The villain's rule; by your hand he
Will perish—so 'tis meant to be!...

I may not yield to indiscretion
And say aught more; your destiny
Yourself from this day on you fashion."

Our knight falls at the elder's feet
And in delight his hand he kisses.
The world a bright place seems, and sweet
Life is again; forgot distress is....
But then the sudden joyful glow
His face leaves, and it pales and darkens.
"Do not despair but to me harken,"
The old man says. "I know what so
Disquiets you: you are in fear of
The warlock's love, eh, knight?... Be calm.
The truth is, O my youthful hero,
That he can do the maid no harm.
From sky the stars he'll pluck, I'll wager,
Or shift the moon that sails on high,
But change the law of time and aging
He cannot, hard as he may try.
Though he lets none her chamber enter
And jealous watch keeps at her door,
He is the impotent tormentor
Of his fair captive, nothing more.
While never far from her, he curses
His lot, and soundly—but, my knight,
'Tis time for you to rest: the earth is
Enclosed in shadow; it is night."

On soft moss lies Ruslan, a flame
Before him flickering. He yearns
For soothing sleep, he twists and turns
And flings about—but no, 'tis plain
That sleep won't come. He heaves a sigh
And says: "Nay, Father, sick am I
Of soul and cannot sleep for dreary
And troubled thought. Talk to me, do;
With godly speech, I beg of you,
Relieve my heart: it aches, it's weary....
I make too bold to ask you this;
You, who befriend me, I importune—
Speak! Tell me, confidant of fortune:
Why came you to this wilderness?"

And with a wistful smile replying
To him, the old man says: "Alas,
I have forgot my land!" Then, sighing:
"A Finn am I by birth. It was
My lot to tend the flocks of neighbours,
And I would take them off to graze
In vales on which no stranger's gaze
E'er rested. Carefree midst my labours
Did I remain, and only knew,
Besides the woods and streams, what few
Joys poverty could offer to me....
Alas! Ahead dark days were looming.

"Near where I lived, a lovely flower,
One named Nahina, bloomed; of our
Young maids none lovelier than she
Was there. One morn, a bagpipe blowing,
My flocks I grazed where grass was growing
In lush profusion. I could see
A brook wind 'fore me; by it, weaving
A garland, sat a dear young lass....
Her beauty – ah, 'twas past believing! –
Drew and enchanted me, and as
I gazed at her I knew I'd seen her
Before.... Yes, knight, it was Nahina,
'Twas fate had brought me there. The flame
Of love was my reward for eyeing
The maid thus brazenly; I came
To know a passion self-denying:
All of its bliss, all of its pain.

"Six months sped by.... I thought to win her
And opened up my heart. I said:
'I love thee dearly, sweet Nahina!'
But my shy sadness only bred
Scorn in her who was vain and prideful;
She was indifferent to my lot,
And said, of all my pain unmindful:
'Well, shepherd mine, I love thee not!'

"I was estranged from all, and gloomy
Life seemed. The shady native wood,
The games of shepherds – nothing could

My hurt soothe and bring comfort to me....
I languished.... But the far seas drew me;
To leave my homeland sought I then
And with a band of fighting men
To brave the ocean's winds capricious....
I hoped to win renown and fame
And for my own Nahina claim.
This planned, according to my wishes,
I called upon some boatmen who
Joined with me in a quest for danger
And gold. My land, to war a stranger,
The clash of steel now heard, and knew
The sound of boat with boat colliding....
On, on we sailed, the billows riding,
My men and I, by sweet hope led,
Both snow and water painting red
For ten long years with gore of foes.
As rumour of our prowess spread,
The foreign rulers came to dread
Our forays, and their champions chose
To flee our blades. Yes, fierce and heated
Our battles were, and merry, too,
And with the men we had defeated
Together feasted we. But through
The din of war and merrymaking
I heard Nahina's voice, and for
The sight of her in secret aching,
Before me saw my native shore.
'Come, men!' I cried. 'Did we not roam
The world enough? Time to go home!
'Neath native eaves we'll hang our mail;
Is't not, in faith, for this we hanker!'
And leaving in our wake a trail
Of fear, for Finland we set sail
And in her waters soon dropped anchor.

"Fulfilled were all my dreamings past
That set my lone heart faster beating.
O longed-for moment of our meeting,
O blessed hour, you came at last!
There, at the feet of my proud beauty,
I laid my sword and, too, the booty
Of war: pearls, corals, gold. 'Fore her,

By jealous womenfolk surrounded,
Her one-time playmates, my unbounded
Love making me her prisoner,
Mute stood I, but Nahina coolly
Turned from me, saying with no sign
That she would e'er relent: 'Nay, truly,
I do not love thee, hero mine!'

"I do not like to speak of things
It is pure agony to think of.
E'en now, my son, when at the brink of
I am of death, remembrance brings
Fresh sorrow to my long-numb spirit
And gravely wounds my being whole,
And torn by pain, seared by it, wearied,
I feel the tears down my cheeks roll.

"But hark! In parts I call my home,
Amid the northern fishers lone,
The art of magic lives. The shaded,
Thick-growing forests wrapt in deep,
Eternal silence lie and keep
The secrets of the wizards aged
Who dwell there and whose minds to quest
For wisdom of the loftiest
And weirdest kind are given. Awesome
Their powers are: what was and also
What will be they have knowledge of,
Life can they snuff and foster love.

"And I, love's mad and avid seeker,
In my despair that ne'er grew weaker,
By means of magic thought to start
In proud Nahina's icy heart
Of love for me at least a flicker.
Toward the murk of woodland free
My steps in hot impatience turning,
The subtle craft of wizardry
I spent unnumbered years in learning.
Then were the fearsome secrets, sought
By me with such despair, such yearning,
Revealed to my enlightened thought;
Of charms and spells I knew the power:

Love's aim achieved – O happy hour!
'Nahina, thou art mine!' I cried.
'Now shall I have thee for my bride.'
But once again by fate defeated
Was I and of my triumph cheated.

"Enraptured, with young dreams aglow,
Filled with love's fervour and elation,
I loudly chant an incantation
And on dark spirits call, and lo! –
A flash of light, a crash of thunder,
And magic whirlwinds start awake,
I feel the earth begin to quake,
I hear it hum and rumble under
My feet, and there in front of me,
The picture of senility,
A crone stands. She is bent and shrunken,
Her hair is white, her eye is sunken
And glazed with age, her head is shaking....
And yet, and yet – had I mistaken
Her for another? – Nay, O knight;
Nahina 'twas!... In doubt, in fright
The horrid vision now I measured
With unbelieving gaze, my sight
Mistrusting.... 'Thou! Art thou my treasured
Nahina? Speak!' from me the cry
Burst forth. 'Where is thy beauty? Why
Have the gods changed thee so? Have I
Long, then, from life and love been parted?'
'For forty years!' I heard her say.
'Indeed, I'm seventy to-day!...
But never mind! So are lives charted
And so they pass. Thy spring has flown
And mine has too. We are, I own,
Old, both, but be thou not disheartened
By fickle youth's swift passage. True,
I'm grey, a trifle crooked too,
Less lively and perhaps less charming
Than once I was....' This in disarming
Tones she declared, her voice a squeak.
'Come, do not look, I beg, so tragic....
I am – in confidence I speak –
Like thee become well versed in magic.'

"A sorceress! What had she said!...
Struck dumb was I by the admission
And felt a fool, a dunderhead
For all my store of erudition.

"But worse by far was that the spell
That I had cast worked far too well.
My shrivelled idol flared with passion;
She loved me – loved me to obsession!
Her grey lips twisted in a smile,
In graveyard tones the old hag muttered
The wildest of avowals, while
I suffered silently, in utter
Disgust and loathing, and upon
The ground my eyes kept. She wheezed on,
And though, by fits of coughing shaken,
So was she with her subject taken,
She never stopped. 'My poor heart is
For tender passion born and bliss,'
She croaked. ''Tis love alone I covet
And hunger for. I flame, I burn....
O come to me, for thee I yearn;
I'm dying, dying, my beloved!'

"'Twas lustfully that she, Ruslan,
Was ogling me. Her bony fingers
Caught greedily at my caftan....
There to remain, knight, there to linger
Beside her was sheer agony;
I squeezed my eyes shut, for, you see,
I could not bear it any longer,
And broke away.... 'Knave! Thus to wrong me!'
She yelped. 'A pure maid's life – quite shattered!
Such villainy! For shame! For shame!
As if my love so little mattered!
Alas! I am myself to blame;
You men, I vow, are all the same.
By thy seduction helpless rendered,
To passion wholly I surrendered....
Deceiver! Blackguard! Thou shalt know
What vengeance is, just wait!...'

                              "'Twas so
We parted. In these forests buried

23

E'er since, a hermit's solitary
Life have I led, and of the balm
Of nature tasted, by its calm
And wisdom doctored. I'll not tarry
Long here on earth.... To you alone
Do I impart this; know: the crone
Has not forgot her unrequited,
Scorned passion. In her soul, her blighted
And ugly soul, love's changed to spite;
And that she'll come to hate you, knight,
As she does me, you can be sure.
But be not, I entreat you, frighted:
Grief's bound to pass, 'twill not endure."

The old man's story hungrily
Our knight took in. Enchanted by it,
He sat there rapt and clear of eye,
Untouched by sleep. The night was quiet:
He never heard it winging by.
Now dawn's bright glow the heavens graces....
With rueful smile Ruslan embraces
The mage, and, full of gratitude,
The cave leaves in a hopeful mood.
He leaps into the saddle deftly,
Grips with his legs the whinnying steed,
And with a whistle moves off swiftly.
"Be with me, Father, in my need!"
He cries. "Farewell!" Across the clearing
The answer carries, his heart cheering:
"Forgive your bride and love her, heed
My counsel, knight! Farewell! Godspeed!"

CANTO THE SECOND

You whose swords clash in contest gory,
Persist in your dread rivalry;
Pay tribute full to sombre glory
And relish hate and enmity!
Let the world, gaping at your deadly
Encounters, freeze – know: none will try
To interfere; more – none will, sadly,
Of pity for you breathe a sigh.
You who compete in different fashion,
Of the remote Parnassian heights
The mettlesome and valiant knights,
Fence if you must, but with discretion,
From vulgar bickering refrain:
The herd 'twill only entertain.
And as for you, by tender passion
Made bitter rivals, pray remain
On cordial terms – for he who's fated
To win a maid's love this will do
Though all mankind should lay plans to
Keep the two lovers separated....
Why fume? – It's silly and a sin.

When bold Rogdai, his heart with dim
But chilling boding filled, had parted
From his companions three and started
Across a lonely tract of land,
As he rode swiftly o'er the woody
And silent plain, on his ills brooding,
The hapless youth could ill withstand,
So troubled were his thoughts, so painful,
The Evil Spirit's taunting baneful,
And whispered: "Smite I shall and kill!
Beware, Ruslan, Ludmila will
Weep over you, I swear!..." And turning
His steed about, down dale, up hill
He galloped, for sweet vengeance yearning.

Meanwhile, Farlaf, that fearless soul,
Had spent in sleep the morning whole,
And then, from noon's hot rays well sheltered,
Beside a brook himself he settled
To dine and thus to fortify
His moral fiber. By and by
He saw a horseman in the mead
Toward him charging. Disconcerted,
The knight with quite uncommon speed
His food and all his gear deserted,
His mail, his helmet, and his spear,
And 'thout a backward glance went flying
Off on his horse. "Stop, wretch, you hear!"
The other cried, to halt him trying.
"Just let me catch you, and you're dead –
I'll make you shorter by a head!"
Farlaf, who found the voice belonged
To bold Rogdai, his rival, longed
The more – quite wisely – to be gone
And his horse lashed and goaded on.
So will a rabbit, danger scenting,
Stop short, and, to escape attempting,
Ears folded, by great leaps and bounds
O'er lea, wood, mound, run from the hounds.
Where passed the chase in all its glory
Spring had the snows of winter hoary
Into great, muddy torrents thawed,
And these at earth's breast ceaseless gnawed.

Farlaf's horse, now a wide ditch facing,
His tail shook mightily, and, bracing
Himself, in his teeth took the bit
And leapt across, nor was a whit
The worse for it. Not so his timid
And far less nimble rider who
Rolled down, head over heels, on to
The mud, and lay there, floundering in it
And waiting to be slain.... Rogdai
Storms up, a wrathful vision. "Die,
Poltroon!" he roars, and his sword raises,
But then is brought up short; his gaze is
Fixed on his foe. Farlaf! Dismay,
Surprise, vexation, rage display
Themselves on his face. His teeth grinding,
He swears aloud. We see him riding
Away in haste, inclined to laugh
Both at himself and at Farlaf.

Soon on a pathway upward winding
He met a hag with snowy hair,
A feeble, bent old thing. "Go there!"
She quavered, "That's where you will find him!"
And with her staff she pointed north.
Rogdai felt cheered; nay, more – elated.
Quite unaware that death awaited
Him up ahead, he started forth.

And our Farlaf? Upon his bed
Of mud we see him breathless lie.
"Where has my rival gone? Am I
Alive," he asks himself, "or dead?"
Then suddenly from overhead
A voice comes – it is hoarse, deep-sounding....
"Rise, stalwart mine, all's calm around you,"
The crone says. "Here's your charger; you
Need fear, good youth, no dangers new."

At this the knight crawled slowly out
And looked around him in some doubt.
Relieved, he uttered sighing deeply:
"I do believe I got off cheaply....
The Lord be thanked! No broken bones!"

"Ludmila's far away," the crone's
Next words were, "and though we be tempted
To try and find her, to attempt it
Is most unwise.... No, no," she drones,
"We'll not succeed: too many hurdles,
And, all in all, to roam the world is
A rather risky enterprise;
You'd soon regret it. I advise
You to go straightway home to Kiev;
On your estate your days you'll spend
In ease, behind you danger leaving –
Ludmila won't escape us, friend!"

With this she vanished, and our knight,
The flame of love well-nigh extinguished
And dreams of martial fame relinquished,
Set off for home. 'Twas not yet night,
But any noise however slight,
A rustling leaf, a bird in flight,
A brook's song put him in a sweat.

But let us now Farlaf forget
And to Ruslan turn.... On he races,
Across a wood we see him ride....
In thought he lovingly embraces
His only love, his fair young bride.
"My wife," he cries, "my own Ludmila,
Will e'er I find you, dear one, will I
Your gaze full of enchantment meet
And hear your tender voice and sweet?
Say, is it in a wizard's power
You are, and is the early bloom
Of youth to fade? Are you to sour
And wither in a dungeon's gloom?...
Or will one of my rivals seize you
And bear you off? – Nay, love, rest easy:
My head is on my shoulders still,
And this my sword I wield with skill."

One day at dusk Ruslan was riding
Along a steep and rocky shore,
The stream below in shadow hiding,
When with a whine an arrow o'er
His head flew, and behind him sounded

The clang of mail, the heavy pounding
Of hooves, a horse's piercing neigh.
"Halt!" someone shouted. "Halt, I say!"
The knight glanced round: far out afield,
With spear raised high and ready shield,
A rider galloped whistling shrilly.
Ruslan, his heart with anger filling,
His steed turned speedily about
And charged toward his grim assailant
Who met him with a brazen shout:
"Aha, I've caught you up, my gallant!
First taste of steel, then seek your fair!"
Now, this Ruslan could little bear;
He recognized the voice and hated
The sound of it. "How dares he! I'll—"

But where's Ludmila? For a while
Let's leave the two men; we have waited
Quite long enough, 'tis time to turn
To our dear maid now and to learn
How she, one lovely past comparing,
Has at her captor's hands been faring.

A confidant of wayward fancy,
Not always modest have I been,
And this my narrative commencing,
Dared to describe the night-cloaked scene
In which our fair Ludmila's charms
Were from her husband's eager arms
Whisked off. Poor maid! When, quick as lightning,
The villain with one movement mighty
Removed you from the bridal bed,
And like a whirlwind, skyward soaring,
Through coils of smoke charged on, ahead,
Toward his kingdom's mountains hoary,
You swooned away, but all too soon
Recovered from that welcome swoon
To find yourself, aghast, dumfounded,
By lofty castle walls surrounded.

Thus—it was summer—at the door
Of my house lingering, I saw
The sultan of the henhouse chasing
One of his ladies, and moved by

Hot passion, with his wings embracing
The flustered, nervous hen.... On high
A grey kite hovered, old marauder
Of poultry-yards; in rings o'erhead
He slowly sailed, unseen; then, boldly,
With lightning speed, dropped down, a dread
And ruthless foe, his plans death-dealing
Laid earlier.... Up soars he, sealing
The fate of his poor, helpless prey.
Clutched in his talons, far away
He bears her to the safety of
A dark crevasse. In vain, with fear
And hopeless sorrow filled, his love
The rooster calls: he sees her airy
And weightless fluff come drifting near,
By swift, cool breezes downward carried.

Like some dread dream, oblivion
Ludmila chains. She cannot rise
And, in a stupor, moveless lies....
The soft, grey light of early dawn
Revives her, deep within her rouses
Unconscious fear and restlessness;
Sweet thoughts of joy her heart possess,
For surely her beloved spouse is
Nearby!... "Where are you, dear one? Come!..."
She whispers, and – is stricken dumb.
Where is your chamber, my Ludmila?
Poor, luckless maiden, you lie pillowed
Upon a lofty feather-bed;
On silken cushions rests your head;
The canopy that floats above you
Is tasselled, rich, and like the cover,
Patterned most prettily. Brocade
Is everywhere, and winking, blazing
Gems likewise. From fine censers made
Of gold rise balmy vapours hazy....
But 'tis enough! This pen of mine
Must fly description – by another
Was I forestalled: Scheherezade.
And no house, be it e'er so fine,
Affords you any pleasure, mind you,
Unless your love is there beside you.

Just then, in garments clad air-thin,
Three comely maidens tiptoed in.
With bows for the occasion suited
Ludmila mutely they saluted,
Then one, of footstep light, drew near
And with ethereal fingers plaited
Her silken locks, a way, I hear,
Of dressing hair that has outdated
Long since become. Upon her head
A diadem of fine pearls setting,
She then withdrew. With softest tread
The second maid approached; 'thout letting
Herself glance up, all modesty,
In sky-blue silk Ludmila she
Gowned quickly, and her golden tresses
Crowned with a mist-like veil that fell
About her shoulders. There—how well
It shields her, with what grace caresses
Charms for a goddess fit; her feet

Encased are in a pair of neat
And dainty shoes. The third maid brings her
A pearl-incrusted sash; unseen,
A gay-voiced songstress ballads sings her....
But neither shoes, nor gown, nor e'en
The pearly sash and diadem
The princess please; no song delights her,
Indifferent she stays to them;
In vain the looking-glass invites her.
To eye her new-found finery
And revel in its wealth and splendour –
The sight seems almost to offend her:
Her gaze is blank; sad, silent she.

Those who love truth and like to read
The heart's most secret book, must know
That should a lady, plunged in woe,
In spite of habit or of reason,
Oblivious of time or season,
Into a mirror through her tears
Forget to peek – well, then she is
In a most grievous state, indeed.

Ludmila, left alone again,
Uncertain what to do, beneath
A window stands and through the pane
Drear, boundless reaches, wondering, sees.
On carpets of eye-dazzling snow
Her gaze rests; filled is she with sadness....
Before her all is stark white deadness;
The peaks of brooding mountains show
Above the silent plains, and, sombre,
Seem wrapt in deep, eternal slumber:
No wayfarer plodding slowly past,
No smoke from out a chimney trailing,
No hunter's horn resounding gaily
Over the snow-bound, endless waste....
Only the rebel wind's wail dismal
At times disrupts the calm abysmal,
And etched against the sky's bleak grey,
The nude and orphaned forests sway.

Despairing, tearful, poor Ludmila
Her face hides in her hands, unwilling

To think of what may be in store....
She pushes at a silver door
Which opens with a sound most pleasing;
Before her, with their beauty teasing
The eye, spread gardens that surpass
King Solomon's in loveliness,
And e'en Armide's and those that to
Taurida's prince belonged. The view
Is one of trees, green arbours forming
And swaying gently; in the air
Of myrtle floats the sweet aroma;
Palms line the paths, and bays; with their
Proud crowns the mighty cedars boldly
The heavens brush; agleam with golden
Fruit are the orange groves; a pond
Mirrors it all.... The hills beyond,
The vales and copses by the blaze of
Spring are revived; the wind of May
Sweeps o'er the spellbound leas in play;
In song melodious and gay
A nightingale its sweet voice raises;
Great fountains upward, to the sky,
Send sprays of gems, then down, enwreathing
The statues that, alive and breathing,
Around them stand. If Phidias' eye
On these could rest, he, though by Pallas
And by Apollo taught, would, jealous,
His magic point and chisel drop....
In swift and fiery arcs that shatter
'Gainst marble barriers which stop
Their headlong downward plunge and scatter
The tiny motes of pearly dust,
The waterfalls cascade, while just
A few steps farther out, in nooks
By thick trees shadowed, rippling brooks
Plash sleepily.... The vivid greenness
Is by the whiteness here and there
Flecked of the lightly-built pavilions
That offer shelter from the glare....
And roses, roses everywhere!...
But comfortless is our Ludmila,
What round her lies she does not see;
The magic garden does not thrill her

With all its sensuous luxury....
She walks all over, where she's going
Not caring; more – not even knowing,
But weeping copious tears, her eye
Fixed sadly on the merciless sky....
Then suddenly her gaze grows brighter,
And to her lip her hand flies lightly:
Despite the sparkle of the morn
A frightening thought in her is born....
The dread way's open: death waits for her –
Above a torrent, there before her,
A bridge hangs 'twixt two cliffs. Forlorn
The hapless maid is and despondent,
She looks upon the foaming stream,
Her tears grow ever more abundant,
She strikes her heaving breast – 'twould seem
She is about to jump – but no,
We see her pause ... and onward go.

Time passes, and Ludmila, weary,
(Too long has she been on her feet)
Feels her tears drying as the cheering
Thought comes that yes, it's time to eat.
She drops down on the grass, looks round her,
And lo! – a tent's cool walls surround her....
The gleam of crystal! A repast
Is set before her, unsurpassed
In choice of food. The gentle sound of
A harp steals near. But though at this
She marvels, our young princess is
Still not at peace, still sorrow-hounded.
"A captive, from my love torn, why
Should I not end it all and die?"
Thinks she. "Oh, villain, you torment me
Yet humour me: such is your whim,
But I ... I scorn you and contempt
Your wily ways. This feast you sent me,
This gauzy tent wherein I sit,
These songs, a lovelorn heart's outpouring,
Which, for all that, are rather boring, –
In faith, I need them not a whit!
'Tis death I choose, death!" And repeating
The word again, the maid starts... eating.

Ludmila rises; in a twinkling
Gone are the tent and rich repast;
The harp is silenced, not a tinkling
Disturbs the calm.... On walks she, past
The greening groves and round them wanders,
While high above the wizard's gardens
The moon appears, of night the queen,
And in the heavens reigns supreme.
From every side soft mists come drifting
And on the hilltops seek repose.
Our princess feels inclined to doze,
And is by some strange powers lifted
As gently as by spring's own breeze
And carried through the air with ease
Back to the chamber richly scented
With rose oil, and put down again
Upon the couch where, grief-tormented,
She lay before. And now the same
Three youthful maidens reappear
And, round her bustling, they unfasten
Hooks and the like of them and hasten
To take her raiments off. They wear
An anxious look; of mute compassion
Their aspect leaves a faint impression
And of a dull reproach to fate.
But let's not tarry more: 'tis late,
And fair Ludmila is by tender
And skillful hands by now undressed.
Robed in a snowy shift that renders
Her charms more charming still, to rest
She lays her down. The three maids, sighing,
Back out with bows, the door is shut.
What does our captive? – Lies there, but
Shakes leaf-like, and, sleep from her flying,
Feels chilled and dares not breathe. Her gaze
Bedimmed by fear, she moveless stays
And tense, with all her being trying
To penetrate the voiceless gloom,
The numbing stillness of the room;
Her heart throbs wildly, fitfully,
An agitated, endless thrumming....
The silence seems to whisper; she
Hears someone to her bedside coming

And in her pillows hides, and oh!—
The horror of it—footsteps.... No!
It cannot be, she must be dreaming.
The door swings open; there's a flare
Of light, and silent, pair by pair,
A file of Moors, their sabres gleaming,
Steps in with even, measured stride.
A look most grave and solemn wearing,
On downy pillows they are bearing
A silver beard. Puffed up with pride,
A pose assuming grand and stately,
Behind it marches in sedately
A hunchbacked dwarf, chin high. It is
To him the beard belongs. On his
Clean-shaven pate a tall, close-fitting
Tarbush, wound round with cloth, is sitting.
He nears her, and Ludmila, led
By shock and fright, flies off her bed
And at him, and his cap she clutches,
And lifts a shaking fist, no doubt
To try to shield herself. And such is
The shriek the poor maid now lets out
The Moors are deafened by't, while paler
Than his fair captive turns her jailer.
He makes to flee, half turns about,
Claps hands to ears in desperation,
And trips, a victim of frustration
And umbrage, on his beard, falls to
The floor, gets up, falls down anew,
Is quite entangled.... In a dither
His dusky menials all are. Hither
And thither rush they, shout and push,
Then, flushed, confused, a wee bit angered,
They bear him off to be untangled
And quite forget the dwarf's tarbush.

But what of our young hero? Pray
Remember the unlooked-for fracas.
Your pencil, quick, Orlovsky! Make us
A sketch of that night-shrouded fray.

The moon shines down upon a cruel
And savage match. Incensed, the young
Combatants fight their bloody duel

'Thout respite. Their great lances flung
Are far from them, their swords lie shattered,
Likewise their shields, their mail is spattered
With blood.... And yet the gory joust
Goes on. Beneath them, waging battle,
Their steeds whip up dark clouds of dust.
In an embrace of steel the two
Bold knights are locked (they're on their mettle),
But seem quite moveless, as if to
Their saddles welded. Rage and ire
Their limbs turn stiff. A liquid fire
Sweeps like a torrent through their veins;
They're intertwined; chest 'gainst chest strains—
But now they weaker grow, they tire;
'Tis clear that soon one of them must
Go under, by the other bested.
Ruslan with iron hand a thrust
To his fierce rival gives, and, wresting
Him from the saddle, lifts him high
Above himself and never falters
But hurls him down into the waters
That seethe below them, shouting "Die!"

I'm sure, my friends, you've guessed aright
With whom my brave and gallant knight
His duel fought. Of battles deadly
The seeker rash it was, Rogdai.
The hope of Kiev, darkly, madly
Ludmila loved he and was by
This led to seek his rival. On
A Dnieper bank it was he found him:
Persistence and resolve had won!
Alas! The hero's strength unbounded
Deserted him, and in the wild
He met his end, was then beguiled
By a young mermaid who caressed him,
And to her icy bosom pressed him,
And, laughing, drew him down at last....
For many years thereafter, when
Night came and o'er the heavens cast
Its sable shroud, his ghost, appearing
There on the bank or in a clearing,
Would frighten lonely fishermen.

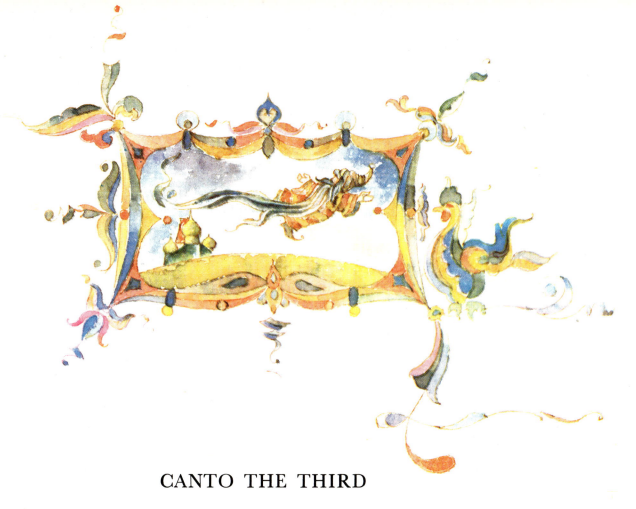

CANTO THE THIRD

You tried to stay from all eyes hidden
Save friendship's own, my verse — in vain!
To envy's scrutiny unbidden
Are you subjected all the same.
A mindless critic has already
The ticklish question asked me, why,
As if to mock Ruslan, his lady
I have been calling "maid".
                        Now, I
Appeal to you, my good, kind reader,
Does not with his lips malice speak?
Come, Zoilus, come, sly-tongued schemer —
What fitting answer can I make?
Blush, wretch, and God be with you, argue
With you I'll not, my heart is free
Of tainted thought, and silent, mark you,
I stay, kept so by modesty.
Dull Hymen's victim, you, Climène,
Will understand; yes, I can see you
Gaze downward languidly, for me you
Feel deeply, sweet.... A tear falls, then
Another on the lines my pen

Has scribbled; clear are they, I know,
To hearts like yours; you flush, the glow
Fades from your eye, your muted sigh is
Most eloquent – a time of trials
Is nearing.... Quake, O jealous one!
For wilful Love with Anger mated
A plot lays – yes, well may you frown:
Your brow inglorious is fated
To boast revenge's twin-horned crown.

A cold dawn gilds the finely chiselled
Tops of the hills.... There reigns throughout
Grim silence. Sulkily the wizard
In dressing gown and still without
His cap, sits on the bed, and, yawning,
Seems angered by the glow of morning.
His dusky slaves, close to him pressing,
Are busy with his beard, a comb,
A fine one, made of walrus bone,
Through all its curvings gently passing.
To give them strength and beauty, they
Pour balm upon his termless whiskers,
And, using curling irons, briskly
Make waves in them.... The calm of day
Is broken – through the window sailing,
A dragon comes; it clangs its scaly,
Well furbished armour, folds its wings,
Coils swiftly into shiny rings,
And suddenly, to the surprise
Of all, takes old Nahina's guise.
"Hail, brother mine!" says she. "I knew you
Till now by loud report alone,
But never grudged you, be it known,
The high esteem and honour due you.
Now secret fate has joined us two
In enmity. The threat of danger
Hangs like a dark cloud over you,
While I'm to be the sole avenger
Of slighted honour, mine, my own;
Its voice I heed."

       The dwarf, a wily
Look on his face, in unctuous tones
Makes his reply: "I value highly," –

To her he now extends his hand –
"Divine Nahina, our alliance.
We'll easily the Finn withstand;
I fear him not at all, for mine is
The greater strength; he ill compares
With me, I vow. This beard I wear,
Grey though it is, has special powers,
And no bold knight, no foe of ours,
However brave, no mortal can,
Unless by hostile force 'tis severed,
Upset my least design or plan;
Ludmila will be mine forever.
As for Ruslan, to die he's doomed!"
"To die! To die!" the witch repeated
With catty spite. "To die!" she boomed.
And then, her mission thus completed,
She hissed three times, thrice stamped the ground,
And flew, a dragon's shape regaining,
Off and away, with vengeance flaming.

In fine brocade most richly gowned
And by the old witch cheered and heartened,
The wizard to the maid's apartment
Anew decided to repair
And take his silken whiskers there
And lovelorn heart. We see him going
From room to room, he passes through
A row of them, vexation growing.
Where is his fair young captive? To
The park he hastes at first, then makes for
The grove, the waterfall, the lake shore,
The arbours, but, dear reader mine,
Finds of the princess not a sign.
By this he's driven nearly frantic,
We hear him moaning, raving, ranting;
He pants, he shakes in every limb,
The light of day's obscured for him.
"Here, slaves!" he splutters, in a flurry.
"The maid is lost! She's disappeared!
Be off with you, you idlers, hurry!
If she's not found, with this my beard,
I jest not, I will have you strangled.
Beware!"

But let us leave the angered
Dwarf, reader, and I'll tell you where
Our maid has gone.... All night she pondered
Her fate, of danger well aware,
But as she wept she ... smiled. You'll wonder
Why so.... She'd met the dwarf, and he,
Despite the beard that she so hated,
Seemed a mere clown, and, you'll agree,
That fear and laughter are ill-mated.
Ludmila rises as the dawn
Is born, and morning's rays creep nearer,
Her sleepy gaze unconscious drawn
Toward a lofty, shining mirror.
Instinctively she lifts her tresses
From lily shoulders, o'er them passes,
As habit tells her to, her hands
And plaits the silky, golden strands.
The garments that she has been given
Lie in a corner. With a sigh
She starts to dress, is newly driven
To quiet tears, but keeps an eye
Upon the faithful glass wherein
She sees herself. A sudden whim
To put the dwarf's hat on now seizes
The princess. It is always fun,
Now, is it not, to try things on,
The very thought is one that pleases!
Besides, by none can she be seen,
And, what is of no smaller matter,
There is no hat that will not flatter
A girl who's only seventeen!
And so the wicked midget's hat
Ludmila turns this way and that;
Straight, then askew she makes it sit,
Down on her eyebrows pushes it,
Claps it on front-to-back.... Behold!
A miracle!—In times of old
They happened often, it appears—
Ludmila's image disappears,
Gone is she from the glass completely;
But in a moment, as she neatly
Turns the hat round, she's there again!
Once, twice she tries it, and the same

44

Thing happens. Cries the princess: "Splendid!
My troubles now are all but ended.
So much for you, vile dwarf, your hunt
For me is over!" And, cheeks glowing,
Herself to be in safety knowing,
She puts the hat on back-to-front.

For shame! Too long has our attention
Been claimed by beard and hat of late;
Our hero giving up to fate,
Of him – alack! – we made no mention.
His duel with Rogdai behind him,
He passes through a lonely wood,
And in a sunlit dale we find him
His stallion reining in. A mood
Of sudden, awful dread comes o'er him:
An ancient battlefield's before him,
And grim it looks, for everywhere
Gleam yellow bones, and here and there
Old, broken armour lies, corroding;
A quiver and a rusty shield
Rest near at hand; far out afield
Stiff, bony fingers hold a moulding
Green sword, a skull is seen to rot
Within a weed-grown helm. And what
Is that ahead? A skeleton,
That of a knight, still armed and on
His fallen, fleshless charger seated,
As if alive and undefeated.
Entwined with ivy, arrows, lances,
Spears from the earth stick. Not a sound
Disrupts of these forlorn expanses
The haunting silence and profound;
The sun alone the vale invades
Of death and of its lingering shades.

Sad-eyed the knight around him gazes.
"O field, wide field, you bear the traces
Of slaughter," says he with a sigh.
"Who planted you to bones and why?
By whose fleet stallion were you trampled?
What bloody battle here was fought
With perseverance unexampled?

Who prayed here and salvation sought?
Why are you mute, why with the grasses
O'ergrown of cold oblivion?
Is there escape from it for none?
Is it that time all, all erases?
What if upon some nameless hill
I am to lie? Mayhap Bayan
Will never chant of me or on
My deeds dwell...."

                      Thus thought he until
It came to him, and this most clearly,
That what he needed – needed dearly –
Was armour and a sword, the night
Of combat having left him quite
Unarmed, alack, or ... very nearly.
On this intent, he walks around
The battlefield where bones lie scattered
And armour, time- and weather-battered,
To see if something can be found.
A sudden clank! A rousing clatter!
The plain from numbing sleep awakes.
A helmet and a shield, the latter
At random picking up, he takes,
And then a ringing horn, but no
Sword to his liking finds, although
Scores of them strew the field of battle:
Being no puny modern knight,
Young Prince Ruslan declines to settle
For one he thinks too short or light.
The boredom fearing of inaction,
A steel lance chooses he for play,
Puts on a hauberk for protection,
And, thus arrayed, goes on his way.

The flames of sunset, slowly paling,
Fade o'er an earth embraced by sleep.
From out the mists the heavens veiling,
A golden moon is seen to creep.
The steppe grows dimmer, nighttime's hazes
Float over it; the path looms dark.
As our young knight rides on, his gaze is
Drawn by a huge black mound, and – hark! –

A fearsome snore comes from't. Our hero,
Undaunted by it, rides up nearer:
The strange mound seems to breathe. Ruslan,
Quite unperturbed, looks calmly on.
Not so his steed, who balks at making
Another step and stands there quaking
With bristling mane and twitching ear
In quite ungovernable fear.
But now the pale orb born to range
The sleepy skies, lights up the nightly,
Mist-covered plain and mound more brightly,
A sight revealing wondrous strange.
Can pen describe the like?... A Head,
A living Head is there! In slumber
Its eyes are shut, it snores, is dead
To all the world, but every rumble,
Each breath and wheeze that from it comes
The helmet stirs and sends the plumes
That reach the shadowed heights a'swaying.
Above the gloomy plain and greying,
The wasteland's guard, in all its chill
And frightful splendrousness it towers,
An awesome hulk, part of the still
And fearful night, possessed of powers
Weird, menacing.... Ruslan decides
To rouse it, and, his eyes half doubting,
Around the Head he slowly rides.
Here is the nose! Without dismounting,
The nostrils with the tip of his
Sharp lance he delicately teases.
The great face puckers up at this;
The great Head, eyes now open, sneezes!...
A whirlwind starts, dust swirls, the plain
Rocks mightily and rocks again,
As if by a convulsion shaken.
The whiskers, lashes, eyebrows rain
Whole flocks of owls. The groves awaken.
The echo sneezes. Shocked, the steed
Lets out a neigh and rears.... Indeed,
He all but throws the knight. A bellow
The air rends: "Back, you foolish fellow!
I jest not. Come and get your due:
I gobble malaperts like you!"

Ruslan, provoked, looks round, and, reining
His horse in sharply, laughs in scorn,
To make a tart retort disdaining.
"Was ever such a nuisance born!"
The Head declares (its tones are surly).
"Sent here by fate to try me, were you?
What do you want? Make off! Adieu!
I'm going back to sleep." "Not you!"
The prince exclaims, these rude words hearing,
And, filled with anger and disgust,
Says: "Silence, empty pate! A just
Truth is it, one not said in vain:
A massive dome, a pygmy brain!"
And then he adds in accents searing:
"I ride along and no grudge bear you,
But cross my path, and I won't spare you!"

At this, the Head, by such cheek numbed,
To a most awful rage succumbed.
It swelled, it flamed, its pale lips trembled,
Turned paler still, were flecked with froth,
Its eyes two balls of fire resembled,
Great clouds of steam now poured from both
Its ears and mouth. And then it started,
Cheeks puffing up, with all its might
To blow at our hapless knight.
To no avail the horse, much startled,
Head downward held and eyes squeezed tight,
To push through rain and whirlwind strained;
Half-blinded, terrified, and drained
Of half his strength, he spun around
And ran, for safer places bound.
Ruslan made fresh attempts to guide him
And to attack the Head anew –
He was repulsed, at him it blew
And cackled crazily. Behind him
He heard it boom: "Ho, knight, where to?
To flee is most unwise of you,
You'll break your neck! Come, my assailant,
Attack me, show me just how valiant
You are! But no, you'd better stop;
Your poor old nag is fit to drop!"
And sticking out its tongue, it taunted

And teased the knight. The monster's leer
Left our young hero quite undaunted
Though sorely vexed. He raised his spear
And at the Head the weapon flung,
And, quivering, the brazen tongue
It pierced and there was to remain
Stuck fast in it. Of blood a torrent
Poured from the maw. The great Head's pain
And its amazement were apparent;
Gone was its cheek, its beet-red hue;
Upon the prince its great eyes fastened,
It chewed on steel, and greyer grew,
And though still seething, was much chastened.
So on the stage one of the Muse's
Less worthy pupils sometimes loses
His head, a sense of where he is
When deafened by a sudden hiss.
He pales, he quakes, what he is there for
Well-nigh forgetting, with an effort
Declaims his lines and ... stops, unheard
By the derisive, jeering herd.
Our gallant knight, the huge Head finding
To be thus discomposed and dazed,
Flew hawk-like toward it, hand upraised
And in a heavy gauntlet cased,
And dealt the giant cheek a blinding
And crushing blow. There starts an echo
That carries o'er the gloomy plain.
The dewy grass is richly stained
With bloody foam. For nigh a second
The great Head sways and rocks, then, lo!—
It topples, hits the ground below
And starts to roll, the steel helm making
A mighty clatter. But behold!—
A huge sword, glittering like gold,
A champion's sword, there's no mistaking
The look of it, lies where the Head
Lay 'fore its fall. The prince, elated,
Now seizes it, and the ill-fated
Head follows, by the fierce wish led
To lop its ears and nose off. Routed
It lies before him, he's about to
Bring down the sword when a low plea,

A faint moan stops him. Startled, he
Lets his arm sink, his ire subsiding,
And ruth, not wrath his actions guiding.
As in a vale snow quickly thaws
When touched by midday's sunshine flaming,
So supplication trims the claws
Of vengeance, its brute powers taming.

"You brought me to my senses," sighing,
The Head now said in accents lame.
"Your right hand proved beyond denying
That I have but myself to blame.
I promise you, I will obey you,
But mercy, mercy, knight, I pray you!
For grim has my plight been; I too
Was once a valiant knight like you,
By none on battlefield excelled
Or to lay down my arms compelled.
And happy I—were't not for my
Young malformed brother's rivalry!
For Chernomor, that fount of hatred,
Alone my downfall perpetrated!
A bearded midget and a stain
Upon our family's good name,
For me who was both tall and straight
He felt a bitter jealousy,
But hid his all-consuming hate
Behind an outward courtesy.
Alas! I have been simple ever,
While he, this wretch of comic height,
Is diabolically clever
And full of viciousness and spite.
Besides—I quake as I confess this—
That fancy beard of his possessed is
Of magic powers: while whole it stays,
That true embodiment of evil,
The dwarf, is safe from harm. With base
Intentions but in accents civil
To me one fateful day he said:
'I need your help.' (There's no refusing
Such an appeal.) 'You see, perusing
A book of magic once, I read
That where rise mighty hills, and breakers

Against them smash, in a forsaken
Stone vault, known to no human, lies
A magic sword that was created
By baneful spirits. Fascinated,
I studied hard and learnt the meaning
Of secret words, in this wise gleaning
A truth to great fears giving rise:
That this sword, so the skies portend
And fate wills, both our lives will end
By parting us, my friend and brother,
Me from my beard, you from your head.
We must procure the sword, none other,
And 'thout delay'. 'Well, well,' I said,
'What's stopping us? We need not tarry!
You'll point the way out. Come, now, hurry,
Get on my shoulder, brother mine;
On to the other one a pine
I'll hoist. If need be we will go
To the earth's very end.' And so
Upon our way at once we started,
And, God be thanked, as if to spite
The soothsay, all at first went right,
And those far mountains, happy-hearted,
I reached at last and went beyond,
And there the secret dungeon found,
And with my bare hands broke it open
And drew the sword out, always hoping
That fate would merciful remain.
But no! We quarrelled once again.
The cause? – O'er which was to possess it,
No mean reward, I must confess it.
He raved, I reasoned, so it went
Until the wily one, while seeming
To yield his ground and to relent,
Devised, to work my ruin scheming,
A knavish ruse. 'Enough! This sparring,
This shameful tiff, life's pleasures marring,'
Said he with solemn mien, 'must cease.
Is it not better to make peace?
Whose sword this is to be, I'm thinking,
Fate can decide. We'll each an ear
Put to the ground, and if a ringing
Should yours reach first, why, brother dear,

You will have won it.' And, so saying,
He dropped on to the ground, and I,
I followed suit and lay down by
His side.... Ah, knight, there's no gainsaying
I was a dolt, a knucklehead,
A perfect ass to have believed him –
I told myself I would deceive him
And was myself deceived instead!
The ugly wretch stood up, and, stealing
On tiptoe to me from the back,
The sword raised. Dastardly attack! –
It sang, a death-blow to me dealing.
Ere I could turn, my poor head was
No longer in its place, alas.
Preserved by some dark, occult force,
It lives (which is no boon, of course),
But all the rest of me, unburied,
Rots in a place to man unknown;
With blackthorn thickly overgrown
My frame is; by the midget carried
I (just the head) was to this spot
And left to guard – ignoble lot! –
The magic sword. For ever after
It shall be yours, 'tis only right.
Fate's kind to you; should you, O knight,
The dwarf meet, be he e'er so crafty,
Avenge me – with this great sword smite
The ruthless knave, my heart relieving
Of all its suffering and grieving.
The juicy smack you gave me I
Will then forget, without a sigh
Or a reproach this sad world leaving."

CANTO THE FOURTH

Each morning as I wake from slumber
To God I tender heartfelt praise
That of magicians nowadays
There is a marked decrease in number,
And that they render now far less
Precarious our marriages.
In fact, their spells need not be dreaded
By those of us but newly wedded.
But there is witchery and guile,
Blue eyes, a tender voice, a smile,
A dimpled cheek, and all the rest,
Which to avoid, I find, is best.
The honeyed poison they exude
Intoxicates; I dread, I fear them.
Like me beware of staying near them,
Embrace repose and quietude.

O wondrous genius of rhyme,
O bard of love and love's sweet dreaming,
You who portray the sly and scheming
Dwellers of hell and realms divine,
Of this inconstant Muse of mine
The confidant and keeper faithful!

Forgive me, Northern Orpheus, do,
For recklessly presuming to
Fly after you in my tale playful
And catching in a most quaint lie
Your wayward lyre....

              My good friends, I
Know that you heard about the evil
Old wretch, the hapless sinner who
In days of yore sold to the devil
His own soul and his daughters' too;
Of how through charity and fasting
And faith and prayer sincere, long-lasting
And penitence without complaint
He found a patron in a saint;
How, when the hour struck, he died,
How his twelve daughters slept, enchanted.
Stirred were we, yes, and terrified
By visions strangely darkness-mantled,
By Heaven's wrath, the Arch-fiend's fury,
The sinner's torments. With enduring
Delight and joy, let us confess,
We eyed the chaste maids' loveliness,
Walked with them, sad of heart and weeping,
Around the castle's toothy wall,
Or stayed beside them, vigil keeping
O'er their calm sleep, their peaceful thrall.
We called upon Vadim, exhorted
Him to come soon, and when the blest,
The holy ones awoke, escorted
Them to their father's place of rest.
Yet had we been deceived and dare I
The truth speak and misgiving bury?...

Ratmir goads his steed on, his way
Toward southern plains impatient making,
Filled with the hope of overtaking
Ludmila 'fore the end of day....
The crimson skies turn slowly darker
And vainly with his gaze he strains
To pierce the haze that cloaks the plains
And sleepy stream. A last ray sparkles
Above the wood and paints it gold.

By nighttime's dark, thick veil enfolded,
Our knight rides past black, jutting boulders....
Oh, for a place to sleep!... Behold!—
A vale before him lies, an old
Walled castle perching high above it
Upon a cliff top; shadow-covered,
At every corner turrets show.
With all a swan's glide, smooth and slow,
Along the wall there walks a maiden;
By twilight's faint ray lit is she,
And on the soft air dreamily
Her song floats, in the distance fading:

"Night cloaks the lea; from far away
The chilling winds of ocean carry.
Come, youthful roamer, do not tarry;
Take shelter in our castle, pray!

"The nights in languid calm we spend,
The days in feasts and merrymaking.
Come, youthful wanderer, attend
This fête of ours, to joy awaking.

"We many are and beauties all;
Our lips are soft, our speeches tender.
Come, youthful wanderer, surrender
And heed our joyous, secret call!

"For thee, O knight, at birth of morning
A farewell cup of wine we'll fill.
Heed thou our summons with a will,
Our gentle plea refrain from scorning.

"Night cloaks the lea, from far away
The chilling winds of ocean carry.
Come, youthful roamer, do not tarry,
Take shelter in our castle, pray!"

He hears her in this manner greet him
And hastens, tempted, to the gate
Where other fair maids, smiling, wait,
A throng of them come out to meet him.
Their eyes to his face glued, they seek
To make him welcome. How entrancing
Their speeches are, .the words they speak!...

Two of them lead away his prancer.
The castle enters he; en masse
The fair young hermits follow. As
One of his winged helm relieves him,
Another 'thout his armour leaves him,
A third removes his sword and shield.
The garb of warfare's bound to yield
To flimsier dress. But first the splendours
Of a true Russian bath wait for
The wayworn youth. In torrents endless
We see the steaming water pour
Into the silver tubs; it eddies
And swirls; swift fountains upward send
Sprays that the warm air coolness lend,
A breezy freshness; all's made ready
To please and gratify the khan.
Rich are the rugs that he lies on!
Transparent wisps of steam curl o'er him;
The maids, all half-nude loveliness,
Around him crowd, a mute caress
Hid in their downcast eyes, and for him
Care with a wordless tenderness.
Above him one waves birch twigs that
Send off sweet scents, another, at
His side stays put and waxes busy,
The juice of spring's fresh roses using
To cool his weary legs and arms
And drown in aromatic balms
His curly locks. Ratmir, enraptured,
Forgets Ludmila, long since captured,
And her once dreamt-of, longed-for charms.
With languor filled and with desire,
His roving eye agleam, he burns,
All passion, and, his heart afire,
For love and its fulfilment yearns.

But now the baths he leaves, and, wearing
Rich velvets, to a feast sits down,
With the young sirens gladly sharing
The wonders of the board. I own
I am no Homer to be singing
In lofty verse (not mine his pen)
The feasts of Grecian fighting men

And their great goblets' merry ringing.
No, like Parny I would that my
Imprudent lyre might tender sigh
O'er love's sweet kiss and sing the praises
Of nude forms dimmed by night's soft hazes!...
Lit by the moon the castle is;
I see a chamber where, reclining
Upon a couch, Ratmir sleeps, pining
For love in dreamy languor. His
Once pallid brow and cheeks are flaming,
His lips, half-open, are aglow
And seem to be in secret claiming
Another's lips; he heaves a low,
A moan-like, lingering sigh, and, seizing
The quilt, with quickened, fevered breathing,
To his breast presses it.... The door
Squeaks open, moon beams streak the floor,
A maid steals in.... Awake, Ratmir!
Of sleep asunder tear the meshes!
Night's every moment is too precious,
Pray waste them not!... The maid draws near
The sleeping knight with softest tread....
His face, on hot down pillowed, blazes,
The silk quilt's slipped from off the bed.
She holds her breath and at him gazes,
Entranced by what she sees, by this
Limp, sensuous form now left 'thout cover:
She's sanctimonious Artemis
Beside her youthful shepherd lover.
Then, gracefully and lightly she
Puts on the couch a rounded knee,
And o'er the lucky sleeper leaning,
Sighs deeply, to his breathing listens,
And rouses him from sensuous dreaming
With passionate and fiery kisses....

But stay! Beneath my slowing fingers
The virgin lyre now turns still,
My shy voice weaker grows—we will
Leave young Ratmir, I dare not sing of
Him more or in this vein go on:
'Tis time, friends, to recall Ruslan,
That stalwart staunch as he is fearless,

That lover true, that gallant peerless.
Exhausted by the mighty fray,
Beneath the Head he now lies sleeping,
But early morning's shining ray
Already o'er the sky comes creeping,
And turns the Head's thick locks in play
To molten gold. Our young knight, blinking,
So sharp's the light, from earthen bed
Springs quickly up, and in a twinkling
By his swift steed is onward sped.

The days run on, the fields turn yellow,
The leaves drop from the trees' bared crowns;
The autumn wind's fierce whistling drowns
The winged songsters' music mellow.
The nude brown hills are daily haunted
By heavy fogs, for winter's near.
But our young gallant knows no fear
And, by its icy breath undaunted,
Heads northward. Daily now he meets
Fresh barriers: now bravely fights he
Another knight, now beats a mighty
And awesome giant, now defeats
A crafty witch. One night he even
As in a dream saw mermaids sit
On swaying, mist-clothed branches lit
By silver moonbeams. Closer driven,
He watched them, full of wonder. They
Said ne'er a word, but smiling slyly,
Tried to enchant and to beguile him.
By kind fate shielded, fast away
The stalwart rode: they could not win him,
Desire soundly slept within him;
To find Ludmila was his goal:
For he was hers—hers, heart and soul.

Meanwhile, kept from the dwarf's advances
Safe by the hat that she has on,
Annoyed by no unwanted glances,
For thus arrayed, she's seen by none,
What does Ludmila?... Silent, teary,
She walks the garden paths alone
And pines for Prince Ruslan, her dearly
Beloved spouse; then, to her home

In far-off Kiev her thoughts flying,
She brightens and, no longer sighing,
Embraces father, brothers, sees
Her youthful playmates in her dreams
And her old nannies; separation
And thralldom suddenly forgot,
She's back among them all; but not
For long does her imagination
Bear her away with it, and soon
Anew is she immersed in gloom....
As for the lovesick villain's minions,
His orders wordless they obey
And search the castle, the pavilions.
The grounds 'thout respite night and day.
They shout, they rush about insanely,
But all, let us admit it, vainly,
For being an accomplished tease,
The maid provoked them without cease.
Before them suddenly appearing,
She'd call out happily, "Yoo-hoo!"

And spotting her as well as hearing
Her voice, the slaves, a motley crew,
Would run to catch her only to
Seize upon empty air; her tinkling
Laugh sounded as the cap she drew
Down on her head, and in a twinkling
Was gone.... Where she had passed, they knew,
For signs of it, however fleeting,
Were to be seen: from off a tree
Ripe fruit might vanish, grass might be
Left crushed and limp; that she'd been eating
Or drinking or else resting there
They could not help but be aware.
A cedar or a birch provided
The maid with shelter; on a bough
She'd perch and try to doze, but how
Could sleep come to a maiden blinded
By endless tears, her heart grief-torn!...
Against a tree trunk weakly leaning,
She might sigh wearily and yawn
And fall a prey to fitful dreaming....
But when the new-born light of day
Night's shadows drove away, and pearly
The skies turned, 'neath the fall's cool spray
She'd wash. The dwarf, one morning early,
Saw, upward forced by hands unseen,
The water play, then join the stream....
Till darkness had anew descended
And moonbeams the lone gardens combed,
Of spirit sore, by none attended,
Ludmila its far reaches roamed.
At times the echoes would be bringing
Her sweet voice closer, softly singing.
Threads from a Persian shawl, a leaf
Chewed through, a tear-stained handkerchief,
A garland by her quick hands made
Might be found lying in a glade.

His passion and frustration mounting,
All else save his piqued pride discounting,
The dwarf has but a single thought:
That the young princess must be caught.
Thus did famed Lemnos' hobbling smith,

Accepting the connubial wreath
From the unrivaled Aphrodite,
Decide to snare her charms, delighting
The laughing gods by showing them
Of love the cunning stratagem.

One day the maid sat bored and weary
Inside a marble summer-house
And gazed abstracted through the boughs
Of trees by wind swayed at the cheery,
Bloom-covered meadow just beyond.
"My love!" she hears. Ruslan! The sound
Of his dear voice. He's there, in person:
His face, his form; but dull of eye
And pale is he, he bleeds, his thigh
Is gashed: a wound, a bad one. "Mercy!
Ruslan, 'tis you!" And with a cry
She flies to him, and, heartsore, shaking,
In tears, says to him, her voice breaking:
"Ruslan, my husband, you are here
And wounded, bleeding.... Oh, my dear!"
Her arms go round him.... God in Heaven!
What horror's this! She cannot stir,
She's trapped, a net enmeshes her!...
The cap falls off. Who is her craven
And foul pursuer? Cold of limb,
She hears: "She's mine!" Her gaze grows dim....
The dwarf, none other! Quite defenseless
Is she again; she sees his face
And moans, but by the good Lord's grace
Dreams now enfold her, she falls senseless.

Poor child! What sight is there more chilling,
More certain to provoke our rage!
His brazen hand the puny mage
Lays on the charms of young Ludmila.
Is he – foul thought! – to taste of bliss?
But hark! A horn sounds. What means this?
A challenge to him? Yes! The midget's
Face shows cold fear. He quails, he fidgets....
A louder blare! Back on her head
The magic cap he puts, and, paling,
Is off, his beard behind him trailing,
To meet the fate that lies ahead.

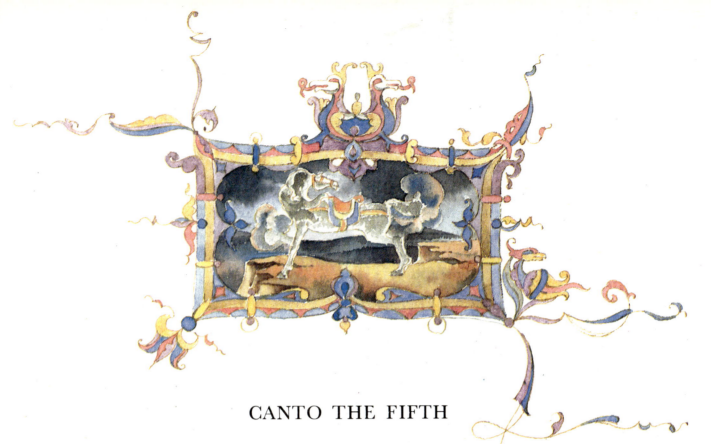

CANTO THE FIFTH

How dear my princess is, one bows
'Fore her, to sing her praises anxious:
She is so tender, unpretentious,
So faithful to her marriage vows;
Capricious, yes, but not unduly,
Which makes her only sweeter, truly.
Her ways delight us, they endear
Her to us, leaving us enchanted.
How to compare her with Delphire
Who's so unfeeling, so flint-hearted!
By fate endowed has been the first
With mien and manner most beguiling;
To hear her speak, to see her smiling
Makes one's heart throb, with love athirst.
Delphire now, spurs and whiskers added,
Would make a true Hussar. But stay!
Blest is he who at end of day
Has a Ludmila waiting for him
In some lone nook, and from her hears
That he's her love, that she adores him.
And likewise blest is a Delphire's
Admirer who is too clear-headed
To court her long and runs away.
But let's not stray too far. Come, say,
Who was it that the dwarf invited

So daringly to fight him? Who
Defiantly the trumpet blew
And by its sound the villain frightened? —
Ruslan. Afire with vengeance, he
Has reached the midget's castle. See?
Beneath the palisades he's halted;
The trumpet's sound comes storm-like, loud,
The steed paws at the snowy ground;
The prince awaits the dwarf. A bolt of
What seems like thunder deafens him.
A crushing blow! It has descended
Upon his helmet. Though defended
By this his head is, yet with dim,
Dull sight it is he upward gazes
And sees the dwarf above him fly,
A mammoth bludgeon lifted high.
Ruslan bends down, his great shield raises
And waves his sword, but Chernomor
Sweeps upward; then, appearing o'er
The prince again and downward swooping,
He flies straight at him, whereupon
The latter feints, his rival duping,
And down the midget falls, straight on
The well-packed snow, with fear nigh frozen.
Ruslan dismounts, and, never pausing,
The space between them neatly cleared,
Grabs the magician by the beard!
The captive grunts and strains, and, heaving
Himself from off the bank of snow,
Sails skyward with our hero, leaving
The knight's astonished steed below.
They're 'neath the clouds, Ruslan still gripping
The beard and swinging in the air.
O'er seas and forests, o'er the bare
And rugged hills, their summits tipping,
The dwarf wings, and the stalwart knight,
Though numb and stiff his hand is growing,
Holds dogged on. The dwarf is quite
Used up by now and winded. Slowing
His progress through the air at length,
Amazed and awed by Russian strength,
He turns to our young knight and slyly
Says to him: "Prince, I'll do you ill

And half-dead wizard stuffs in haste,
The dancing steed no longer staying,
And starts uphill. The top. They ride
Up to the massive palace portal.
Ruslan – there is no happier mortal –
In hot impatience steps inside.
The throng of Moors and slave girls, seeing
His helm with beard graced, know the knight
To be the victor and are fleeing
Before him, fading out of sight
Like ghosts. Ruslan from hall to hall
Strides all alone; we hear him call
To his young spouse – the echo answers....
Is she not in the necromancer's
Great castle, then? The garden door
He opens wide, all expectation,
And on walks fast. His eye sweeps o'er
The empty grounds in agitation:
All's dead, naught stirs, still are the groves,
The leafy arbours and the coves;
The river banks, the slopes – deserted,
The valleys too.... He's disconcerted,
For nowhere e'en a trace is there
Of her he seeks, nor can he hear
The slightest sound. There passes through him
A sudden chill, the world grows dark
About him, and bleak thoughts come to him:
"Captivity.... of grief the mark....
A moment, and the waves –" These fancies,
How dismal they! His head hung, he
Stands like a rock there movelessly....
His very reason clouds, his senses
Fail him. He's all ablaze, he flames;
Despairing love's dark poison surges,
A mighty torrent, in his veins.
Is't not his lady who emerges
From darkness, is't not she who clings
To him?... He roars her name, he flings
Himself about, and, frenzied, raving,
His sword in mad abandon waving,
At boulders strikes and makes them roll
Downhill, and hacking, mowing, slashing,
Pavilions to the ground sends crashing,

Reduces grove and lea and knoll
To barren wastes, and tumbles bridges
Into the streams. The distant ridges
Send back the clang, the boom, the din;
Ruslan's sword sings and whistles. Grim
The scene is: all is devastation;
Insensed and maddened, our young knight
A victim seeks; on left and right
His sword the air cuts 'thout cessation....
Then all at once a chance thrust sends
The midget's magic headdress flying
From off his captive's brow; so ends
The spell cast on her. 'Fore him lying,
Enmeshed, Ruslan Ludmila sees.
He does not trust his eyes, he is
O'ercome by happiness, and, falling
At his bride's feet, tears up the nets,
And with his tears her limp hands wets,
And kisses them, her dear name calling.
But closed her lips are and her eyes,
And sensuous are the dreams she's seeing
That make her bosom sink and rise.
Fresh sorrow fills our knight's whole being;
What means this sleep? Is she perchance
To be forever in a trance?...
But hark!–a friend's voice.... 'Tis the Finn,
His councillor, who speaks to him:

"Take heart, O Prince! Upon your way
For home set off with fair Ludmila
And, strength of purpose your heart filling,
To love and honour faithful stay.
God's bolt will strike, defeating malice;
You shall know peace, all will be well.
In Kiev, in Vladimir's palace,
Your bride will wake, free of her spell."

Ruslan, much cheered, no longer weary,
Lifts up his calmly sleeping bride,
And down a slope we see him guide
His horse and leave the mountain eyrie.

The midget to his saddle tied,
Across a vale, across a forest

He hurries, by no rival harassed.
In his arms his love rests, a precious
And welcome burden. Oh, how fresh is
Her face! The vernal dawn can be
No more so. 'Gainst her husband's shoulder
It rests, all sweet serenity....
The wind born in the barrens boldly
Plucks at her silky golden hair.
She sighs, the roses on her fair
Young cheeks play. Her beloved's name
She whispers; 'tis her dreams that bring her
His image and her heart inflame;
On her lips love's avowals linger.
And he – he's all fond contemplation
(The sight of her his spirit cheers) –
Oh, that sweet smile, those glistening tears,
That lovely bosom's agitation!...

Meanwhile, by day, by night they journey
Up hill, down dale, but still unspanned
The distance is, still far the land
Which to behold Ruslan is yearning.
The maid sleeps on.... Did our young knight,
By fruitless, unassuaged desire
Worn – for it seems like years – not tire
Of guarding her? Did he delight
In virtuous dreams, immodest longing
Subduing and in no way wronging
His drowsy charge? So told are we
By one, a monk, who put in writing
The story of the prince, inviting
Inquisitive posterity
To profit by't. And I – I fully
Believe the annalist, for, truly,
What's love unshared? – An irksome thing
That can but little pleasure bring.
Ludmila's sleep did not resemble
Yours in the least, nymphs of the mead,
When languid springtime's call you heed
And in the cooling shade assemble
Of leafy trees.... I well recall
That happy day in early summer,
A tiny glade at evenfall,

And lovely Lida feigning slumber....
That kiss of mine, so light, so shy,
So hurried, young love's fresh, sweet token,
Could not awake the maid; unbroken
It left her sleep.... But, reader, why
Do I talk nonsense? Why this needless
Remembrance of a love long dead?
Forgot its joys, its pain, its heedless
And trying ways. To speak I'm led
Of those not long from my thoughts gone:
Ludmila, Chernomor, Ruslan.

A vale before them spreads; upon it
Rise clumps of spruces, and a mound
Looms farther out, its strangely round
And very dark and gloomy summit
Against the bright blue sky outlined.
Our youthful knight at once divined
That 'twas the Head before them showing;
The steed speeds on, more restive growing;
Across the plain its great hooves thunder....
And lo!—they're close, they're nearly there;
Before them is the nine days' wonder,
It fixes them with glassy stare.
It is a thing repulsive, horrid:
Its inky hair falls on its forehead;
Drenched of all life, the hue of lead
Its face is, while the huge lips, parted,
And, like the cheeks, of colour bled,
Disclose clenched teeth; over the Head
Its hour of doom hangs. Our brave-hearted
And doughty knight rides up and faces
Its sightless gaze; the midget graces
The horse's rump. "Hail, Head!" Ruslan
Cries loudly, for the Head to hear him.
"He who betrayed you is undone!
Look! Here he is, none now need fear him!"
These words the Head revivified
And in it roused new, fresh-born feeling.
It looked down at them, and, revealing
All of its anguish, moaned and sighed.
Our hero it had recognized,
And at the midget, nostrils swelling,

Stared, full of venom undisguised.
A fiery red its pale cheeks turned,
And in its death-glazed eyes there burned
A fury fierce and all-compelling.
In towering rage, incensed, confused,
It gnashed its giant teeth, and stuttered,
And smothered imprecations muttered,
And with its slowing tongue abused
Its hated brother.... But the pain,
Prolonged as it had been, was ceasing;
The dark, flushed face turned pale again,
And weaker grew the heavy breathing.
Its eyes rolled back, and soon Ruslan
And magus knew that all was over:
A spasm, and the Head was gone.
The knight rode off at once, much sobered;
As for the dwarf, he did not dare
To breathe, and, all his past strength losing,
To fiends in hell addressed a prayer,
The language of black magic using.

Where a small nameless streamlet wound,
Upon the sloping bank above it,
By dark and shaded forest covered,
There stood, nigh sunk into the ground,
A run-down hut. Thick pine-trees shaded
Its roof. The waters, somnolent,
Licked lazily at a much faded
And worn-down fence of reeds and went
With gentle murmur round it snaking;
The breeze blew softly, only making
A faint sound.... There it was that spread
A vale, and such was its seclusion,
It gave one the distinct illusion
That an unbroken silence had
Here from the birth of Time been reigning.
Ruslan now stopped his horse. The waning
And peaceful night to morn gave way;
The grove and valley sparkling lay
'Neath veils of haze. His sleeping bride
The prince laid on the grass, and, seating
Himself beside her, close, he sighed
And looked at her, his young heart beating

With dulcet hope. Just then a boat's
White sail he glimpses, and there floats
A fisher's song above the water
That drowns its gentler voice and softer.
The man has cast his nets, and, bending
With zeal and promptness to the oar,
His humble vessel now is sending
Straight for the hut perched on the shore.
The good prince shades his eyes and watches:
There now — the boat the green bank touches,
And from the hut there hurries out
A sweet young maid; her hair about
Her shoulders loosely falls, she's slender
And bare of breast, her smile is tender,
She's charm itself. The two embrace
And on the bank sit, taking pleasure
In one another, in this place,
And in a quiet hour of leisure.
But whom to his intense surprise
Does Prince Ruslan now recognize
In this young fisherman? Dear Heaven!
It is Ratmir! Yes, it is he,
A man for exploit born, and even
For fame itself, one of his three
Sworn rivals. On this halcyon shore
He turned to fair Ludmila faithless,
And for his new love's warm embraces
Relinquished fame for ever more.

Ruslan came up to him, astounded;
The recluse khan his rival knew.
A cry, and to the prince he flew
And joyous threw his arms around him.
"You here, Ratmir? Lay you no claim
To greater things?" our hero asked him.
"Have you found life like ours too tasking
Thus to reject your knightly fame?"
"In truth, Ruslan," replied the khan,
"War and its phantom glory bore me;
Behind me have I left my stormy,
Tumultuous years. This peace, this calm,
And love, and pastimes innocent
Bring me a hundred-fold more gladness.

My lust for combat being spent,
No tribute do I pay to madness;
Rich am I, friend, in happiness,
And have all else forgot, yes, even
Ludmila's charms." "I'm glad, God bless
You for't, Ratmir, for fate has given
Her back to me...." "You have your bride
With you!" amazed, the young khan cried.
"What luck! I too once longed to free her....
Where is she, then? I'd like to see her —
But no! I'll not betray my mate;
Made mine by a forgiving fate,
She wrought this change in me, the fervour
Of eager youth in me revived;
Because I'm hers, because I serve her
I know true love and am alive.
Twelve sirens who professed a longing
For me without regret I spurned;
My heart to none of them belonging,
I left them never to return;
I left their merry home, a castle
That in a shaded forest nestled,
My sword and helm laid down, and foe
And fame forgot. 'Twas, my friend, so
That, peace and solitude embracing,
A kithless hermit I became,
And dwell, to no one known by name,
With her I love...."

                         Upon him gazing,
The shepherdess ne'er left his side;
Now smiled she sweetly, now she sighed....
On, on, unseen, the hours went racing.

Their hearts by friendship warmed, till night
Set in, o'er all its patterns tracing,
The fisher sat beside the knight....
It's still and dark. The half-moon's light,
Pale just at first, is brighter growing.
Time to be off! A cover throwing
With gentle hand o'er his young bride,
Ruslan goes off to mount his steed.
The khan, bemused, preoccupied,

In spirit follows him; indeed,
Good luck in all his daring ventures
He wishes him and happiness
And his proud dreams and past adventures
Recalls with fleeting wistfulness....

Why is it Fortune has not granted
My fickle Lyre the right to praise
Heroic deeds alone? Why can't I
Of love and friendship, that these days
Are out of fashion, chant? A bard
Of Truth, why must I (God, it's hard!)
Denounce spite, venom, vice, am fated
In my sincere and artless songs
To bare for those to come the wrongs
By crafty demons perpetrated?

Farlaf, Ludmila's worthless wooer,
A wretch, still eager to pursue her,
But all his dreams of glory gone,
Out in the wilds lived, isolated
From all mankind and known to none,
And for Nahina's coming waited.
Nor did he, reader, wait in vain:
For here she is, the ancient dame!
A solemn hour. "You know me, stalwart,"
She says to him. "Now mount, and forward!
Come after me." And lo! – with that
She turns herself into a cat,
And then, the charger saddled, races
Off and away. She's followed by
Farlaf on horseback. Through the mazes
Of gloomy forests their paths lie.

Clad in night's haze that never lifted,
The vale lay tranquil, slumber-bound,
And, veiled in mist, the pale moon drifted
From cloud to cloud and lit the mound
With fitful rays. Beneath it seated,
Our hero, staying at her side,
Kept vigil o'er his sleeping bride.
By tristful thought all but defeated
The poor prince was; within him crowded
Dreams, fancies and imaginings;

Beginning gently to enshroud him,
Above him hovered sleep's cool wings.
His closing eyes upon the sweet
Young maid he tried to fix, but, feeling
Unable this to do, sank, reeling,
By slumber captured, at her feet.

A dream comes to him, bodeful, gloomy:
He seems to see Ludmila, his
Sweet princess, pale-faced and unmoving,
Pause on the brink of an abyss.
She vanishes, and he is standing
Above the dreaded chasm alone,
And from it comes, the spirit rending,
A call for help, a piteous moan....
'Tis she! He jumps, and flies apace,
To pierce the darkness vainly straining.
Through fathomless, night-mantled space,
And then, at long last bottom gaining,
Steps on hard ground.... Vladimir's palace
Before him towers.... He enters. There is
The old Prince with his grey-haired knights,
His twelve young sons, his guests, all seated
At festive tables. No smile lights
Vladimir's face. He does not greet him
And seems as wroth as on the dread
And well-remembered day of parting.
All silent stay, no banter starting,
No talk. But there — is not the dead
Rogdai among them, his past rival,
The one that he in battle slew?
Quite unaware of his arrival,
A froth-topped goblet of some brew
He gaily drains. Surprised, Ruslan
Espies Ratmir, the youthful khan,
And others, friends and foes, ringed near him;
The gusli tinkle, old Bayan
Of deeds heroic chants — to hear him
Is strange. Farlaf now enters, leading
Ludmila in. The Prince, receding
Into himself, his grey head bowed,
Says not a word. The silent crowd
Of boyars, princes, knights, concealing

What so disquiets, so dismays
And frightens them, quite moveless stays.
Then, in an instant, all is gone....
A deathly chill o'er his heart stealing,
Ruslan now finds himself alone.
From his eyes tortured tears are flowing,
Sleep fetters him, he tries to break
Its leaden chains, but fails, and, knowing
'Tis but a dream, cannot awake.

Above the hill the moon looms pale;
Dark are the forests; in the vale
Dead silence reigns, and there, astride
His steed, we see the traitor ride.

A glade and barrow he has sighted;
Stretched at his love's feet, on the ground
Ruslan sleeps, and around the mound
His stallion walks. Farlaf, much frightened,
Looks on a'tremble. In the mist
The witch is lost. No signal sounding,
The bridle dropping from his fist,
He rides up closer, his heart pounding,
And leans across, his broadsword bared,
To cleave the knight in two prepared
Without a fight. His presence scenting,
The stallion whinnies angrily
And paws the ground. But what's to be,
There is, I fear me, no preventing!
Ruslan hears nothing, for sleep on him
Weighs heavily, a cruel vise.
Spurred by the witch, Farlaf's upon him,
And plunging deep his sharp steel thrice
Into his breast, his priceless prey
Lifts up and, weak-kneed, rides away.

The hours flew. Beneath the barrow
The whole night long our hero lay;
The blood from his wounds oozed in narrow,
Unending streamlets.... Dawn arrived,
And with its coming he revived,
Let out a heavy, muffled groan,
About him peered, and, vainly trying
To lift himself and stand, fell prone,
Like one already dead – or dying.

CANTO THE SIXTH

You bid me, O my heart's desire,
Take up my light and carefree lyre
And chant the lays of old, my leisure
Devoting to a faithful Muse.
Do you not know, then, that I treasure
Love's raptures more and frankly choose
To spend but little of my time
With that long cherished lyre of mine,
That being now at odds with rumour
And drunk with bliss, I'm in no humour
To welcome toil or harmony's
Sweet, winsome strains.... By you I breathe,
And though loud are fame's prideful speeches,
Their sound my ear but faintly reaches.
Of genius the secret fires
Are dead; its thoughts are left behind.
Love, love alone my heart inspires,
Its wild desires invade my mind.
But you — you'd have me sing; my stories
Of loves long past and erstwhile glories
Appeal to you; you wish to hear
Of Prince Ruslan and of Ludmila,
The dwarf, Nahina, Vladimir,

And to the old Finn's woes a willing
And patient ear are glad to lend.
The tales I spun would sometimes tend
To make you feel a trifle sleepy
Though with a smile you listened e'er.
At other times I was aware
How tenderly – this felt I deeply –
Your loving gaze the singer's met.
Enamored babbler, I will let
My fingers pass over the lazy
And stubborn strings, and at your feet,
The minstrel's customary seat,
Strum loudly, my young champion praising.

But where's Ruslan? Out in the field,
His blood long cold and long congealed,
He sprawls, a raven o'er him swooping,
Upon the grass lie limp and drooping
The whiskers serving to adorn
His helm of steel; mute is his horn.

His golden mane no longer waving,
Around the prince his mount walks gravely,
Head lowered; in his once bright eye
The light has died. Not knowing why
The prince lies so, he is unwilling
To play and waits for him to wake.
In vain! The prince won't move or take
The sword up: deep his sleep and chilling.

And Chernomor? There, in the bag,
He lies, forgotten by the hag,
And knowing naught, his grudges nurses;
Worn, sleepy, bored to tears, he curses
My youthful hero and his bride....
Then, not a sound his ears assailing
For hours on end, he peeps outside –
A miracle, no less! Words fail him.
For in a pool of blood the knight
Lies dead, and no one is in sight;
Ludmila's gone, the field's deserted.
The wizard crows in joy. "I'm free!"
He cries. "All danger is averted."
But he is wrong, as we shall see.

Farlaf, by old Nahina aided,
On horseback makes for Kiev; he
Is full of hope and fear. The maiden
Across the saddle lies asleep.
Ahead, the Dnieper, cold and deep,
Already shows, its waters flowing
Mid native leas; the city's glowing
Gold domes and wooden walls draw near.
Here is the gate! The townsfolk cheer,
And mill about, excitement mounting.
Word to the Prince is sent. Before
The eyes of all, at palace door
We see the knavish youth dismounting.

Meanwhile, Vladimir, called Bright Sun,
Was in his lofty terem sitting,
And, filled with sorrow unremitting,
On his loss brooding. Round him, glum,
His knights and boyars sat, a pompous,
Stone-visaged lot. A sudden rumpus
Is heard without: yells, shouts, a din;
The portal opes. A knight comes in.
Who can he be? Why the intrusion?
All rise. A murmur fills the room,
Grows louder. General confusion.
Ludmila rescued! And by whom!—
Farlaf, of all men! Strange! The Prince,
Changed wholly now of countenance,
Starts from his chair and, heavy-footed,
Hastes to his long-lost daughter's side.
He touches her; she stirs not; muted
Her breathing is. Ruslan's young bride
Rests in the killer's arms unfeeling,
The hands of magic her lips sealing,
Its powers holding her spellbound.
His men the aged Prince watch dully
As, anxious-eyed and melancholy,
Farlaf he queries, though no sound
Escapes him. "Aye, the maiden sleeps,"
A finger holding to his lips,
Without a qualm, Farlaf says slyly.
"I found her, Prince, held by a wily
And wicked goblin captive in
A Murom forest. Bound to win
Was valour, and it did. We battled
For three long days. Above us two
The moon rose thrice; then all was settled:
He fell. The sleeping maid to you
I rushed to bring from that forsaken
And lonely spot. When she's to waken
And with whose help is only known
To fate, whose ways are dark. Alone
Hope, yes, and patient meditation
Can offer us some consolation."

Throughout the town there flew ere long
The fateful news, all hearts distressing.

The square filled with a seething throng
Of townsfolk, toward the palace pressing.
A house of grief, it opes its doors
To all, and there the crowd now pours
To see the youthful princess sleeping
On a raised couch clothed in brocade,
The knights and princes o'er the maid
With sombre faces vigil keeping.
Horns, tympans, gusli, tambourines
And trumpets sound. The Prince, grief-worn,
His grey head 'gainst his child's feet leans
With silent tears. Beside him, torn
By mute remorse, dismay, self-pity,
Farlaf stands trembling, white of face,
His brashness gone without a trace.

Soon darkness fell, but in the city
None closed an eye, and all throughout

The night discussed, grouped near their houses,
How it could all have come about,
Some husbands lingering without
And quite forgetting their young spouses.
But when the twin-horned moon on high
Met dawn, its bright rays slowly paling,
There rose throughout a hue and cry,
A din, a clang of arms, a wailing.
A new alarm! And, shaken, all
Come scrambling up the city wall.
A mist the river cloaks. Beyond it
They see white tents, the glint of shields,
Dust raised by horsemen in the fields,
And moving carts: they are surrounded;
Up on the hilltops campfires flame....
To such scenes Kiev is no stranger;
It's clear the city is in danger,
The Pechenegs attack again!

While this went on, the Finn, a seer
And ruler of the spirits, waited,
Withdrawn from all the world, to hear
Of happenings anticipated,
Foreseen by him.... Calm, tranquil he:
What is ordained is bound to be.

Deep in the steppe, sun-parched and soundless,
Beyond a chain of hills, the boundless
Realm of wild gales and windstorms, where
The aweless witch will scarcely dare
To walk with the approach of evening,
A vale lies hid that boasts two springs:
One leaps o'er stones and plays and sings,
For it is rich in water *living*;
The other o'er the valley bed
Flows sluggishly, its waters *dead*.
All's silence here, no breezes blowing
That coolness bring; no busy bird
To chatter or to sing is heard;
No age-old pines on sand dunes growing
Are seen to stir; no fawn, no deer
Drinks of these waters. It is here
On guard two spirits have been standing

Since Time began, the fear commanding
Of all. Before them now the Finn
Appears, two jugs, both empty, bearing;
Their trance is broken, and from him
They flee, to other parts repairing.
He fills the vessels with the pure,
Sweet water 'fore him softly streaming,
And then is off, to vanish seeming
Into thin air. A second or
Two seconds pass, and in the vale
Where, motionless and deathly pale,
Ruslan lies, he now stands. First he
Dead water o'er the knight sprays, causing
The gaping wounds to heal and rosy
The grey lips turning suddenly;
With living water then he sprays
The comely but still lifeless face —
And death is vanquished, gone its rigor;
Ruslan, full of fresh strength and vigour,
Stands up; life courses in his veins,
The past a ghastly dream remains
Behind him, dim.... O'erjoyed, he faces
The rising day that 'fore him blazes.
But he's alone.... Where's his young bride?...
Of fear a tremor passes through him;
Then his heart leaps, for at his side
He sees the Finn who now says to him:
"It's as Fate wills. Bliss is in store
For you, my son, but not before
A bloody feast you'll have attended
And with your sword put down the foe.
You'll see your bride and gladness know,
Once peace on Kiev has descended.
Here is a ring for you. Her brow
Touch with it, and from sleep she'll waken.
The very sight of you, I vow,
Will leave your foes confused and shaken
And put the lot of them to flight.
Then will maliciousness and spite,
My friend, and all things evil perish.
Be worthy of your love and cherish
Your bride, Ruslan.... And now goodbye....
Beyond the grave will you and I

Meet, not before." With this he vanished,
And Prince Ruslan, all his fears banished,
O'erjoyed to be to life restored,
Stands with his arms stretched out toward
His friend.... Alas! The grassy lea is
Deserted quite save for the bay
(The dwarf's still in the bag) who whinnies
And rears and shakes his mane. Away
The prince now makes to go, and, springing
Into the saddle, grips the reins.
He's hale and sound. Across the plains
And woods we see him boldly winging.

And what of Kiev, by the foe
Beleaguered?... There, filled with suspense,
High on its walls and battlements,
The townsfolk crowd. The fields below
Surveying fearfully, they wait
God's smiting hand, the hand of fate.
Subdued laments come from the houses;
No sound the fear-hushed byways rouses.
Beside his child in earnest prayer
Vladimir kneels, plunged deep in sorrow.
His knights and noblemen and their
Great warrior-host for war prepare:
The bloody fray's set for the morrow!

Dawn broke, and down the hills the foes
Poured, armed with swords and spears and bows;
They surged relentless, never slowing,
Wave upon wave across the plains
And toward the city walls came flowing.
The Kiev trumpets started blowing,
And out its men rushed, with the chains
Of the attackers boldly clashing.
The fray begins! In sudden fear,
As death they scent, steeds neigh and rear;
The riders, forward headlong dashing,
In battle meet, their steel swords flashing.
Sent forth in clouds, the arrows hum;
The fields turn red: with blood they run.
A man who's lost his war-horse faces
A horseman: which of them will smite

The other first? In wild-eyed fright
Across the field a charger races.
Death. Cries for help and battle-calls.
A Pecheneg, a Russian falls.
One's by an arrow pierced swift-flying;
Another's maced, his groan unheard;
A foeman's shield has crushed a third,
And, trampled on, he lies there, dying.
The fray went on till dark set in,
But neither warring side could win....
The slain in mounds lay; blood flowed freely;
Sleep claimed the living, all concealing
From their sight. Through the fearful night's
Long hours the wounded moaned in pain,
And one could hear the Russian knights
To their God pray and speak His name.

But paler turned the shade of morn,
And in the swiftly-flowing river
The rippling waves seemed made of silver:
Day, thickly cloaked in mist, was born.
The hills and forests slowly brightened;
The skies, by sun their blueness heightened,
Broke free of sleep.... Yet moveless still
The battlefield remained until
The hostile camp awoke abruptly,
A challenge followed the alarm,
And warfare once again erupting,
Old Kiev lost its short-lived calm.
All rush to watch the scene below
And see a knight in flaming mail
Through ranks of foemen blaze a trail,
See him descend on them and mow
Them boldly down—see his sword flash
And thrust and stab and cut and slash....
It was Ruslan. The dwarf behind him,
His horn triumphantly he blows
And like a thunderbolt the foes
Strikes down; where'er it is we find him
Borne by his steed, the infidels
Row upon row he vengeful fells,
And awing the enthralled beholders,
With whistling sword parts heads from shoulders....

Where'er he passes, bodies strew
The battleground, crushed, headless, dying,
With spears and arrows near them lying
And heaps of armour. Then, anew
The trumpet's battle call remorseless
Sounds, and behold!–the Slavic forces
To join Ruslan on horseback fly.
A fierce fray follows.... Pagan, die!
The Pechenegs, those savage raiders,
Round up their scattered horses and
In panic flee. The feared invaders
Of Russ, they can no more withstand
The Slavs' attack; their wild yells carry
Over the dusty field; their hordes,
Cut down by Kiev's smiting swords,
The fires of the inferno face....
Kiev exults.... And now our daring
Young prince–his horse he sits with grace–
On through its gate rides, proudly bearing
His sword of victory; his lance
Shines star-like, drawing every glance;
The blood is seen to trickle down
His heavy mail of bronze, he's wearing
A helm whose top the whiskers crown
Of Chernomor. And all about him
There's noise and gaiety and shouting.
The very air with his name rings....
Toward the Prince's house on wings
Of hope he flies, and goes inside.
Here now's the silent chamber where
Sleeps fair Ludmila; at her side
Her father stands, deep lines of care
Etched on his face. There's no one near him,
No friend to comfort or to cheer him,
For they have all gone off to war....
Farlaf, alone the call of duty
Denying, at the chamber door
Kept vigil; in him deeply rooted
Was an aversion for things martial,
To calm and comfort he was partial,
And very much so. Seeing who
Was there before him, he surrendered
To fear; his blood froze; speechless rendered,

On to his knees he fell.... He knew
That retribution was his due,
That he was doomed. Ruslan, however,
The magic ring just then recalled
And, faithful to his love as ever,
Her pale brow touched with it. Behold! –
She oped her eyes and sighed in wonder:
Night had been long, too long.... It seemed
That she was still entranced, still under
The spell of something she had dreamed.
And then her vision cleared – she knew him!
And fell into his arms, and to him
Clung lovingly. By joy made numb,
He saw naught, heard naught, his heart raced....
And Prince Vladimir, overcome,
Wept as his dear ones he embraced.

You will have guessed, and without fail,
How ends my all too drawn-out tale.
Flown was Vladimir's wrath ungrounded;

Farlaf confessed his guilt; Ruslan,
So happy was he, in him found it
All to forgive; the dwarf, undone,
His powers lost, was added to
Vladimir-Bright Sun's retinue;
To mark an end to tribulation
A sumptuous feast of celebration
The Prince held in his chamber high,
By friends and family surrounded.

The ways and deeds of days gone by,
A narrative on legend founded.

EPILOGUE

Thus, the world's mindless dweller, spending
Life's precious hours in idle peace,
Its strings my lyre to me lending,
I sang the lore of bygone days.
I sang, the painful blows forgetting
Of fate that blindly o'er us rules,
The wiles of frivolous maids, the petty
And thoughtless jibes of prating fools.
My mind, on wings of fancy soaring,
To parts ethereal was borne,
While all unknown there gathered o'er me
The dark clouds of a mighty storm....
And I was lost.... But you who always
Watched o'er me in my earlier years,
You, blessed friendship, giving solace
To one whose heart deep sorrow sears! —
You calmed the raging storm, and, heeding
My spirit's call, brought peace to me;
You saved me — saved my treasured freedom,
Of fiery youth the deity!
Far from the social whirl, the Neva
Behind me left, forgotten even
By rumour, here am I where loom
Caucasian peaks in prideful gloom.
Atop high steeps, mid downward tumbling
Cascades and cataracts of stone,
I stand and drink it all in dumbly,
And revel, to reflection prone,
In nature's dark and savage beauty;
To wounding thought my soul's still wed,
Within it sadness lives, deep-rooted,
But the poetic fires are dead,

In vain I seek for inspiration:
Gone is the blithe and happy time
Of love, of merry dreams, of rhyme,
Of all that filled me with elation.
Sweet rapture's span has not been long,
Flown from me has the Muse of song,
Of softly spoken incantation....

FROM THE PUBLISHERS

Written in 1820, when Pushkin was very young, *Ruslan and Ludmila* was his first major work. Its appearance signalled the birth of a genius who was soon to make all of Russia resound with his name. "The sun of Russian poetry", as the poet came later to be called, was rising.

A graduate of the Tsarskoselsky Lyceum, Pushkin, like his fellow students, had a good knowledge of the literature of classicism with its poetic evocation of a past rich in heroic deeds. In *Ruslan and Ludmila*, a poem written in a light and humorous vein and characterized by an easy grace and lucidity, Pushkin saw fit to present this heroic past in a facetious light and to parody the mumbo-jumbo of sorcery and mysticism.

Why the poem, when it was brought out, was met with such sharp controversy, can only be explained by its originality, its complete unorthodoxy. Having chosen for his theme the romantic story of four Russian knights who set out to rescue a princess captured by a wicked magician, the poet introduces a consciously "earthy" approach to it and is quick to ridicule his characters. Ruslan, whose young bride has been carried away from him, is likened to a rooster, "the sultan of the henhouse", Ludmila, to a flustered hen, her captor, Chernomor, to a kite, "a marauder of poultry-yards".

The poem is gay and festive and bubbles with life. The poet makes a confidant of his reader, invites him to join in the fun and to thrust away, as does he, the chains that shackle man's spirit.

REQUEST TO READERS

Raduga Publishers would be glad to have your opinion of this book, its translation and design and any suggestions you may have for future publications.

Please send all your comments to 17, Zubovsky Boulevard, Moscow, USSR.

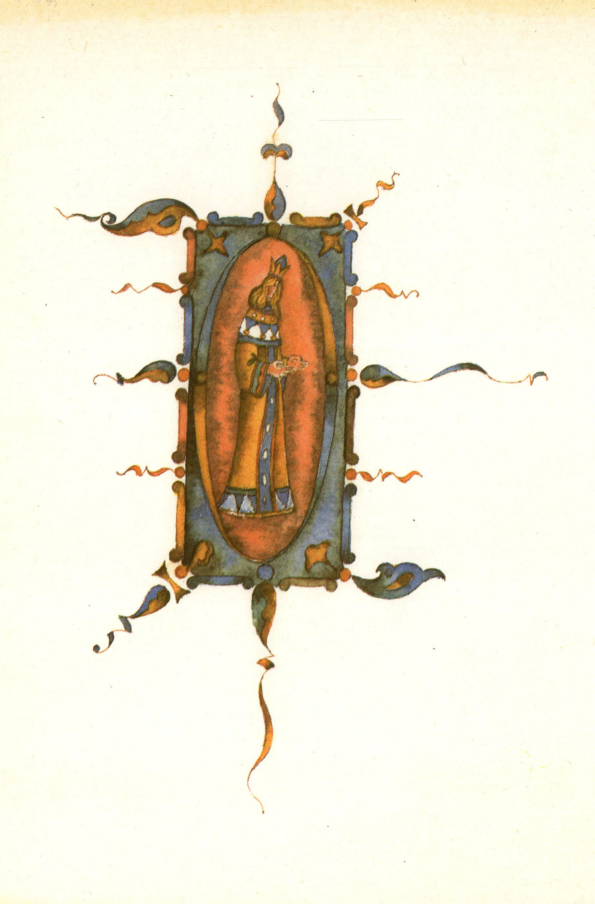